THE YEARS OF

COMING OF AGE UNDER THE KHMER ROUGE

Foreword by Roger Rosenblatt

A sensitive and uplifting tribute to the resilience of the human spirit

SENG TY

Inquiries should be addressed to author by email or website:
yearsofzero@sengty.com
www.sengty.com

ISBN-13: 978-1492286738
ISBN-10: 1492286737
Library of Congress Control Number: 2013917707

First Edition: November 2013

Cover design by: Andrea Brown
Interior layout by: Malisa Kuch

The information in this book is true and complete to the best of our knowledge. All recommendations are made without guarantee on the part of the author or The Years of Zero. The author and publisher disclaim any liability in connection with the use of this information.

Printed in the United States of America

Contents

Foreword

On the other side of the restaurant table, Seng and Sreymom eat their lunch and look at me like expectant children. The couple are in their early thirties. Twenty-two years have passed since I first met Seng at the Khao I Dang refugee camp in Thailand, to which he had escaped from Pol Pot's slaughterhouse. As a man he looks much as he did then—more aware and a little weary, yet still alert, respectful, gentle. His ears protrude like the handles of brown coffee cups. His eyes are dark and searching, like a scholar's. So are his wife's. They met and married in Massachusetts; both of them part of the community of Cambodians who had emigrated to the area around Lowell. Sreymom goes to nursing school. Seng is a guidance counselor. They tell me that they are enjoying their salads.

It is so strange, wonderfully strange, sitting across from Seng in the sun-painted bistro. I met him when I was writing a cover story for *Time* magazine in 1982, called *Children of War*, which later became a book of the same title. Now Seng has written a book about his life in Cambodia, this beautiful book about a terrible time and place. The occasion of our lunch is to celebrate its completion. I realize that I am observing a miracle, two miracles, in a serene French restaurant, in New York, in America, in a world that would have seemed a distant planet to Seng the little boy.

My book, *Children of War*, was about a great many children living in half-a-dozen war zones at the time, yet the publisher deliberately chose the photograph of Seng for the cover flap. The reason, I believe, is that even at the young age of eleven, Seng's face bore a determined dedication to survival, in spite of the killing around him. Seng's father was shot to death by a firing squad because he was a doctor, thus an intellectual, thus an enemy of the state that the Khmer Rouge had made mad. His mother died of starvation a few years later. At the age of eight, Seng oversaw her burial in their village. He was alone in the world. He wrote in his diary, "Dear Friend, I turn to you in my hour of sorrow and trouble."

That was Seng's first book, and this is his latest. In it one finds the description of a country so dangerous and murderous in its efforts at self-destruction, it is astonishing that it ever recovered. The fact that in its recovery Cambodia is still run by former members of the Khmer Rouge constitutes a madness of its own. Yet the people, as Seng portrays them here, have managed to regain a certain humanity. At one point recently, Seng considered returning to Cambodia to live, but he discovered in young manhood that his heart had relocated.

So this is the story of two worlds, much as my lunch with Seng and Sreymom embodies two worlds. Principally, it is the narration of a nightmare, both personal and national, but because it is related by a writer of such goodness and courage, one does not feel as frightened or saddened as one does ennobled. There are terrible moments in this book, and lovely, and even funny ones as well, and they make for a rich and uplifting experience in reading. But the most effective element of the story is its author, in whose character an entire people are rescued.

Seng himself was rescued from the refugee camp because *Children of War* happened to be read by a family in Massachusetts who became his foster parents. Seng was lucky, and so was I; happy consequences of journalism are rare. Only a few years ago did I see him again, grown and purposeful and confident in his adulthood and loving marriage. And yet, as he stood in my doorway, it was clear that the child was father of the man. I would have known him anywhere.

At our lunch, I tell Seng that I have framed the drawing that he made for me at Khao I Dang. It hangs near my writing desk. Twenty-two years ago in the camp, I had asked him if he would do a self-portrait, but instead, he had produced the picture of a bright blue airplane, with a green door, green engines and a nose and tail. I had asked him where he was in the drawing, and he said, "I am the pilot! We are flying to France!" His eyes were wide with hope and excitement, as they are now, as he wonders how his book will be received.

I think I can tell him. It will be received for what it is—a tale of life born of death, unforgettable, indispensable, and his own.

Roger Rosenblatt

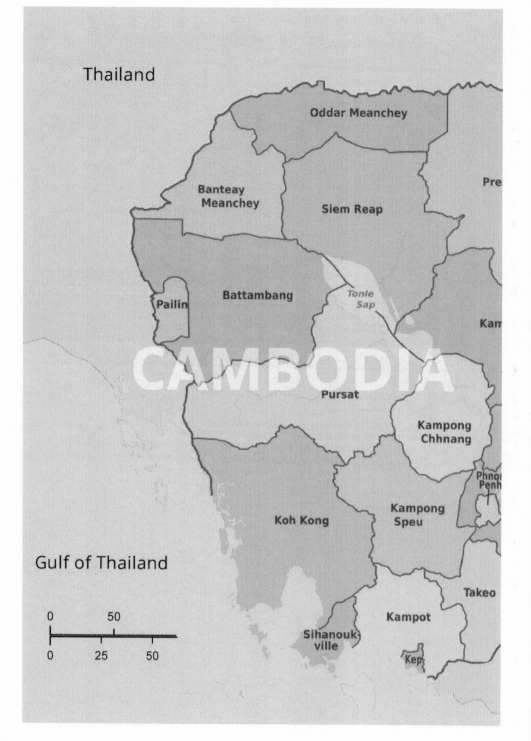

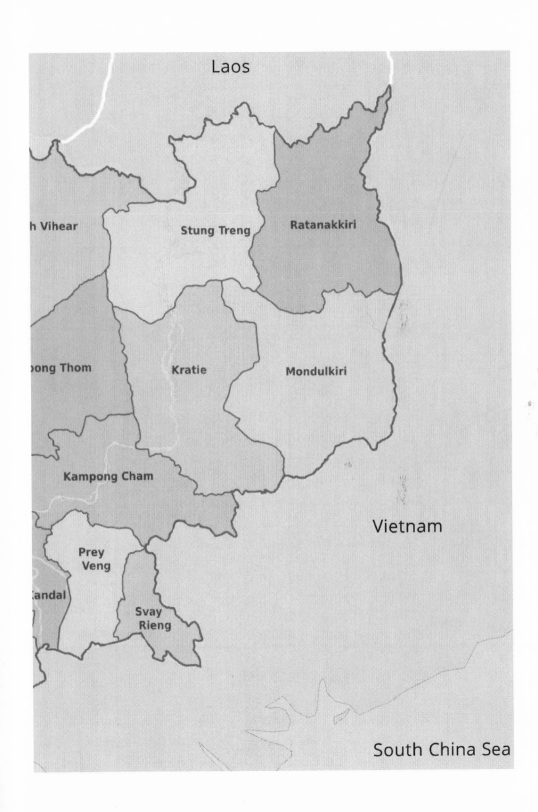

Historical Timeline

Cambodia has a long history. It began when the Khmer Empire was founded by King Jayavarman II in 802 AD (CE). He was a powerful king who established the capital at the temple-city of Angkor (now Siem Reap). From 802 to 1431 AD, the Khmer Empire was the most powerful nation in Southeast Asia, and amassed a great cultural wealth that has been passed down through the generations to present-day Cambodia.

1863   In response to political tensions with Thailand and Vietnam, Cambodia becomes a French protectorate under King Norodom I. French colonial rule would last for ninety years.

1941   Upon the death of his grandfather, the king, Prince Norodom Sihanouk was appointed king by the Vichy French Protectorate in the mistaken belief that the young king would be easier to control than his father. The Japanese occupied Cambodia from 1941 to 1945, at which time they threw out the French government and declared the country the Kingdom of Kampuchea. After the war, the Japanese occupation ends, and Cambodia becomes a French protectorate once again.

1953   King Norodom Sihanouk negotiates independence for Cambodia, abdicates, naming his father king, and becomes President. Sihanouk goes on to rule the kingdom of Cambodia for seventeen years.

1965   King Norodom Sihanouk tries very hard to keep Cambodia neutral as the wars in neighboring Vietnam and Laos escalate. To this end, he agrees to allow Vietnamese communist forces to set up bases in Cambodia in pursuit of their campaign against the US-backed government in South Vietnam. After the US sends troops to Vietnam, Cambodia breaks off relations with the US. The US begins the secret bombing of Cambodia

1969 The United States begins a four-year-long carpet-bombing campaign, devastating the countryside and causing socio-political upheaval for the entire country. Prior to the bombing, the radical communist Khmer Rouge, led by Pol Pot, had been a small fringe group hiding in the mountains, but the bombing reinforced their message that all the ills in Cambodia were caused by western powers, and tens of thousands of peasants flocked to their cause, along with idealistic young university students. The United States eventually dropped more bombs on neutral Cambodia than had been dropped by all parties on both fronts in all of World War II. As a result of the carpet-bombing, a conservative estimate of half a million civilians ware killed or wounded. The US and Cambodia renew diplomatic relations.

1970 Cambodians take to the streets to protest against the presence of North Vietnamese and Viet Cong troops in their country. While King Norodom Sihanouk is out of the country, General Lon Nol, the defense minister, overthrows Sihanouk in a coup which was probably backed by the US Central Intelligence Agency, and which greatly dismayed the US State Department. Lon Nol names himself prime minister, and proclaims that Cambodia is now the Khmer Republic. Sihanouk goes to China and allies himself with the Khmer Rouge, giving their movement much credibility with the Cambodian people. US ground troops enter Cambodia to attack Vietnamese communist bases.

1971 The Republican Army fights the North Vietnamese within Cambodia's borders, and suffers major defeats.

1973 The Vietnamese begin withdrawing, and the Khmer Rouge take over the fighting. The US resumes bombing. Civil War engulfs the country, marked by much corruption on the Khmer Republic side, and fanatical fighting on the Khmer Rouge side.

1975 One quarter of the nation's population is living in Phnom Penh as war refugees flee to the capital, and the Khmer Rouge, represented by five different groups, relentlessly take over the rest of the country.

April 17, 1975, The Khmer Rouge enter Phnom Penh and immediately begin forcing the populace into the countryside, with the intention of creating a new, completely agrarian society. In the final weeks of the war, four of the five Khmer Rouge leaders, known as the Five Ghosts, 'disappear', and Pol Pot is now solely in charge. The country is renamed Democratic Kampuchea, and Prince Norodom Sihanouk becomes titular head of state.

1975–1979 The Years of Zero. The Khmer Rouge declare that "this is the year zero" from which a new history of Cambodia will be created, replacing all the past. No aspect of the old culture is considered valid. Their ultimate goal is to wipe out anyone who can remember a reality different from the one they offer.

1976 Prince Sihanouk resigns as head of state. Pol Pot is declared prime minister of Democratic Kampuchea.

1977 Pol Pot simultaneously launches a purge — arresting and killing many of the Khmer Rouge leaders who had dedicated their lives to his cause — and escalates attacks on Vietnam in an attempt to recover "Kampuchea Krom," the southern section of Vietnam lost to the Vietnamese in the eighteenth century.

1978 Fed up with Khmer Rouge incursions into their territory, Vietnam invades Cambodia in December. The Khmer Rouge have been so weakened by the purges that it takes Vietnam only two months to occupy Cambodia.

1979 Heng Samrin, a former Khmer Rouge official who had fled to Vietnam to avoid being purged, is declared head of the People's Republic of Kampuchea, the new government established by Vietnam. The international community refuses to recognize this government as legitimate, so for the next 10 years, the Khmer Rouge represent the people of Cambodia on the international stage and at the UN. Thailand refuses to allow international aid to the refugees on the Thai border unless aid is given to all groups, and in the ensuing decade, the Khmer Rouge completely rebuilds its strength, and there is constant warfare between them and the Vietnamese and Cambodian armies.

1989 The Vietnamese withdraw, and the country is renamed the State of Cambodia.

1991 A peace agreement is signed in Paris. A UN transitional authority shares power temporarily with representatives of the various factions in Cambodia.

1993 Prince Norodom Sihanouk returns to Cambodia, and is restored to the monarchy. Meanwhile, Cambodia holds its first general election, monitored by the United Nations, with an astonishing 90% voter turnout. The Cambodian People's Party loses the election, but refuses to step down. All elected positions are then shared by two people. The two prime minister's are Hun Sen, of the CPP, and Prince Norodom Ranariddh, Sihanouk's son, of the Funcinpec party.

1997 Hun Sen stages a coup d'état, forcing co-Prime Minister Prince Norodom Ranariddh into exile, and he then controls Cambodia.

1998 Cambodia makes international news; Pol Pot, Brother Number One, leader of the Khmer Rouge, dies in his jungle hideout on the border of Cambodia and Thailand, having been tried, convicted and sentenced to lifelong house arrest by the Khmer Rouge for the murder of his second-in-command along with the man's entire family. (He had previously been sentenced to death in absentia by a Cambodian court).

2006 The Khmer Rouge war crimes tribunal, sponsored by the United Nations finally begins. Those Khmer Rouge leaders still alive are questioned about their involvement during the cruelty and genocide between 1975 and 1979. They all deny any responsibility. The Khmer Rouge tribunal is currently prosecuting the top leaders, who are now in their eighties, for crimes against humanity.

2012 King Norodom Sihanouk dies of natural causes at the age of eighty-nine. Sihanouk was a very popular king in Cambodia, having won independence from France. However, during his seventeen-year rule many educated Cambodians opposed his monarchy, which they felt had destroyed the Cambodian economy.

2013 Brother Number Three, Pol Pot's second-in-command Leng Sary, dies at the age of eighty-seven from natural causes in the middle of his trial. Pol Pot's brother-in-law, he was a core Khmer Rouge leader who had helped lead Cambodia to the Years of Zero and was instrumental in the campaign to recall expatriate Cambodians abroad back home under the auspices of rebuilding their nation, only to have them imprisoned, tortured and killed at Tuol Sleng in Phnom Penh.

ONE

The Blessings

I remember the beauty and peace of Cambodia before the Khmer Rouge. Her people were generous and free-spirited. Her land was fertile, carpeted with rice fields, and her every monsoon a blessing. The sun rose and set in its cycle of time, waking and sleeping, being born and dying. The peasants toiled all day, every day, in the rice fields. By cockcrow, they were out of the houses to plow, weed, or harvest, and only as the sun was about to set did they journey back home to their families.

My birth into the world was a big event for my parents. Father wanted a big family because he had been alone in the world as a child—he had no brothers and sisters and his parents had died young. But Mother was pained by every birth, and I was to be her last. Knowing that, the family celebrated when they brought me home. My brothers and sisters took turns looking at me, a little creature whose cheeks were puffy and pink. Although I don't know the date of my birth, the year was 1968. I was the youngest of eleven children, and we lived in the village of Ang Sarey, Kampong Speu Province.

The countryside was serene, with fields that were flat and low, earthen dikes dividing them into checkerboards. In the mountains, temple monks wore robes of yellow and orange, and thatched village huts were built on stilts. Birds sang and flitted up and down on palm trees, which our district was famous for. They flew over rice paddies and chased one another under a beautiful blue sky. The air itself was dry and cool, and sunrise and sunset were especially beautiful—the sky burned in hues of red, pink, and yellow over green rice fields. I remember seeing young boys returning home on the backs of their water buffaloes, and hearing the music of cowbells in the evening as the cows and oxen were herded from far away. Men whipped the oxen and shouted at them to pull their loads faster. Hardworking women balanced baskets crowded with vegetables on their heads. Children ran around chasing one another. People labored tirelessly in backyard vegetable patches to feed families of ten or twelve, and gathered mangoes, coconuts, jackfruit, longan, guavas, and bananas from backyard trees. My second-oldest brother Da and I would ask our mother for a few riels to buy fresh palm juice, harvested right from the trees. I loved drinking it.

My country is a vast plain with a low mountain range known in English as the Cardamom Mountains. We call them *phnoms*. From our home, I would dream of the mountains, the sun, and the green bamboo bushes that grew along the riverbank. Beyond the backyard, we could see beautiful rice paddies and a few palm trees. As dawn broke, I would hear the cocks crow and feel the serenity of the land as it woke to the sun. I would run and play with my brothers and sisters to the rhythms of nature. By five a.m., my mother woke to her kitchen and the sounds of people washing their faces and brushing their teeth mixed with the sounds of motors and critters, a ritualized peace. At night, the frogs croaked and crickets chirped. It was pure innocence in our big land.

Each year, two seasons controlled the lives of the farmers—the wet and dry seasons. During the dry season, from February to

June, after the rice had been harvested, the wind whispered and the palm trees arched and reached up high. By April and May, it had grown humid and terribly hot. When the monsoons came in September and October, the land was parched and ready for them. By November, the floods subsided and we had our spring, the most beautiful time of year. The temperature was perfect and the rice paddies turned bright green and gold. Lotuses and water lilies grew. The moisture brought mushrooms and dandelions to the surface. Fish, crabs, and frogs multiplied, and the farmers and city people ate well. The scents from the flowers that my mother planted around our house—jasmine, champa, and malis — perfumed the air in the evening and early morning.

Water was vital to Cambodian life. It quenched my thirst, cooked the food Mother prepared, and irrigated the rice fields. Water was a friendly home to the fish we ate. Water meant health and prosperity. It was a treasure, guarded by the mythical snake, Naga, and we gave thanks to Buddha for it.

I took the days for granted because I knew no other world. My family was very happy together. Nothing would ever happen to us. That confidence was the wonderful gift I received from my parents as they cared for me and loved me. Life, as I remember, seemed simple, even though people often struggled to meet their needs.

My mother, like most Cambodian women, assumed the traditional role of a housewife. She cooked and took care of us, while my father, a physician at a local state hospital, worked hard to provide for us. My mother invested some of my father's earnings in farmland, which she rented to farmers. They, in turn, paid us with half the rice they grew. It was a fair bargain. My father respected the farmers, and to make sure that we understood where our food came from, he would point out the people who cultivated the rice fields for us.

When I was one year's old, after celebrating my birthday my parents handed me over, kicking and screaming, to a farming couple they knew who lived about twenty miles away in the coun-tryside. The couple had no child of their own, and my mother asked for their help in rearing me. As she told me later, it was only meant to be for a while.

I was sent to stay with "Mak" (Mother) and "Pa" (Father) in their tiny village on a hill. They saw me as a precious gift from the ancestors and, even though they knew that my parents would take me back some day, cared for me as if I was their own little boy. But that short stay turned into a visit of nearly three years.

It was difficult for me at first, but after a while, their smiles and warmth won over my heart and their tiny thatched house on stilts became my home. I hardly saw or heard the noise of motors or cars there, nor did we have electricity, but life with Mother Mak and Father Pa was safe and peaceful. I played in the rice fields and muddy ground. My white skin turned brown from smearing my face with dirt. My parents visited on weekends with generous gifts of fruit and French sweets.

Then one day when I was about four years old, my mother came to take me away. News had spread of a war that was spilling peasants' blood and she feared for my safety. "You go with your mommy," Mother Mak said. "It's safer there. We'll see you again." I cried and kicked and held on to them so tightly that Mother Mak had to come along to Ang Sarey with me. I remember my real mother taking my hand and thanking the couple for their kindness in caring for me. She told them that if they ever needed to, they could stay with us. Mother Mak went back to the village. I never saw her or Father Pa again.

I missed them, their thatched home, and the animals I was used to feeding and playing with in the afternoon. My real parents, brothers, and sisters offered toys and delicacies to calm me down, but I sat in one spot crying until I fell asleep. I felt very sad and I didn't want to be in this crowded house. It took me some time to call my real parents Mother and Father.

We were a big, middle-class family. Two of my six older

brothers, Lean and Poev, and one of my sisters, Ny, were attending the University of Phnom Penh. My oldest brother, Yean, was attending university in France. My three other sisters, Mohm, Chan, and Theary, were still in high school, as were my next older brothers, San and Reth. My brother Da was two grades ahead of me.

It was always a treat to go into Phnom Penh to see my brothers and sister at the university or to visit friends and relatives. Ang Sarey was about forty miles from the city. That seemed far, but it was close by car. We weren't poor—we had everything we wanted—and in the city, I was surprised to see so many poor people. Some were begging on the street. I remember riding with my mother on the *cyclo*. The man pedaled fast to the market. My mother paid him a few riels for the ride. I enjoyed riding up high, watching people on the sidewalk, the air hitting my face. Little boys in tattered clothes without shoes idled on the street. Mother always pointed them out, to teach us not to forget what we had and to make sure we understood what education could do for our lives.

In every restaurant and in many homes I saw framed pictures of the king and queen on the walls. At family dinner, my parents always said good things about the royal family. In the 1960s, King Norodom Sihanouk had begun to slowly industrialize Cambodia. He brought electricity to much of the country—I remember when my father wired our house and bought light bulbs to replace our kerosene lanterns. My brothers and sisters, who had always read by lamp light, could read more easily with the shiny bulbs. How excited I was to have electricity!

Ang Sarey was only a couple of miles from the provincial market in downtown Kampong Speu. We drove there almost every day along Highway 4, which had been extended and paved with asphalt by the Americans shortly before I was born. We saw more motorcycles, cars, and buses, and fewer oxcarts and bicycles. Food stalls and houses had been built alongside the road. Travelers stopped to eat, chitchat, and visit those they knew along the way.

In the quiet years before the war, I remember my mother's

mornings being full of rituals. She began with prayers, chanting mantras softly to herself and lighting a candle at the family altar in the living room. Both of my parents were Buddhists, and if it was a special day of the Buddhist calendar, they brought flowers, fruit, and money to the temple. They listened to the lectures given by the monks and taught us the Buddhist values of compassion, love, and respect.

After her prayers, Mother would wake up my brothers and sisters for school. My older sisters got up early to help her make breakfast, a traditional duty she wanted to pass on to them. She fed us with vegetables from her garden and with fruit from our mango, coconut, and longan trees. Sometimes she went to the market early with one of my sisters to get fresh fish and meat. She waited for the farmers to bring in their vegetables and fruit. Sometimes she would take me along, and I got to eat dessert or noodles.

What I liked most was having breakfast at home with the whole family. Sometimes we had rice soup or noodle soup. Mother knew that I also had a special fancy for French bread, so she often sent one of my brothers early to get it fresh, when the seller had just taken it out of the oven. When it was still hot, the bread was especially tasty. The best thing the French ever left us was the recipe for their baguettes. I liked having it with a Western breakfast of fried eggs, butter, and cheese.

Education was the number-one priority in our household. Everyone had to attend school and learn. Mother had never been formally taught and she wanted us all to have good educations. She had so much hope for us, especially for Yean, who had gone to study in France when I was about four years old.

I remember the day I entered first grade. I was five years old. My mother gave me a bath in cold water and dressed me in my school uniform of white shirt and blue shorts. My clothes were nicely ironed, my hair well combed. Mother handed me a bag with books that I could not yet read and a small chalkboard on which to practice the Khmer alphabet. With a smile, she sent me off to school just as she had sent each of her other children. She was so happy that her youngest son was finally going to school. She didn't have to babysit me anymore. Now the teacher would do that.

My father drove me to school in his car. He hardly said anything on the way. I couldn't tell whether he was happy or sad. I didn't know whether I should fear or love him. Maybe he was proud. Maybe he was thinking of when he was a child without a father to take him to school. He must have thought how lucky I was to have him catering to my needs. He had always been shy and reserved. Without brothers or sisters, he had to carry the burden of family traditions by himself.

Father had learned how to take care of himself at an early age. He finished high school and graduated with honors from the prestigious University of Phnom Penh, the only university in Cambodia, and was selected by the government of Prince Sihanouk for a fellowship to study medicine in France. Doctors were very much needed, and medicine was one of the most respected professions in the country.

My father went to medical school not because of the prestige, but because he thought he could heal people and make a better world. I knew he was a very kind person because I had seen him help farmers who couldn't afford medical treatment for their children. When peasants began to flee into the city from the countryside because of the war, he gave them emergency care and medicines. Along Highway 4, refugees from the war began to began set up temporary shelters. My parents gave them land and shelter to use until the war ended.

Before and after Cambodia's independence from France in 1954, many Cambodian students studied abroad, mostly in France at first and then, during the Lon Nol regime, from 1970 to 1975, in the United States of America. During King Sihanouk's reign, my father was sent to France to continue his medical training. Western medicine was considered superior, and to be educated in the West was a special opportunity.

With his French education, Father became a much sought-after bachelor among the aristocrats and educated elite in Phnom Penh. His relatives and friends tried to find him a lucky girl to marry. Mother was the one they found. She was beautiful, obedient, and polite. She came from a household of sisters who had all been trained to be good housewives. The men would make money and provide for the family. The rules were clearly defined, and Mother always played her role very well.

From early childhood, my mother had been taught by her mother to be a perfect wife who catered to every need of the family. That was to be her contribution to the world. She kept us clothed, clean, and healthy. She made sure we had enough to eat and water to wash with and drink, and that our house was clean and neat. That was her love. That was her duty. When we were sick, she nursed us back to health. She never complained. Although she'd never received a formal education, she knew how to touch our hearts. I have always thought of her as an angel.

When Cambodia was still a French protectorate, my grandmother on my mother's side worked for a French businessman in the capital. The French had deeply influenced the Cambodian language, culture, and government. They owned land, buildings, rubber and sugar cane plantations, and they'd turned the people of Cambodia into their servants. Because of her years in service, Grandmother had acquired an air of aristocracy. Although she never received any formal education, she spoke Thai, Laotian, Vietnamese, and several different dialects of Chinese, as well as French, and had fashioned herself into a lady of French elegance. She kept everything neat and clean.

The French liked order and beautiful things. They collected antiques and relics to sell for profit, and Cambodia was a country of many ancient ruins and artifacts. With their broad boulevards and colonnaded villas, they made Cambodia a little French tropical city. I remember Grandmother was always bringing us French food that she had learned to cook, French baguettes, and French bonbons. The only thing I developed a taste for was the bread, especially when it was fresh from the oven, hot and crispy.

When the French finally left Cambodia in 1954, my grandmother started her own business—a convenience store—with money she had saved while working as a maid. The business thrived because she spoke so many languages, especially Chinese, the language of trade and bargaining. Grandmother lived in Phnom Penh, where we would visit her from time to time. She told us stories of her travels to neighboring countries as a broker to buy and sell consumer goods. She died when I was still very young, and I don't remember what she looked like, but I do remember she always brought toys for me and my brother Da. We were her favorite grandchildren. Every time she came to Kampong Speu Province, she gathered her grandchildren and told us her favorite folktales and ghost stories. She was an old woman, but she had a lot of energy for bartering, selling, and buying in the market. My mother tried to persuade her to live with us, but she always refused. She enjoyed living on her own among all her friends and regular customers.

My mother, who was less vocal and assertive than my grandmother, was born in the village of Tunie Tuk Meas, Kampot Province. In those days, girls rarely went to school , and Grandmother kept Mother in the house to do chores and help her run the store. Mother was the second oldest of three siblings, Grandmother was a widow, so she needed Mother, the older of her two daughters, to help her around the house. Grandmother raised them all strictly and traditionally, with the dignity she had acquired throughout her life. She wouldn't allow her daughters to go out and socialize with men. Nor were they allowed to choose their own husbands. Parents arranged marriages for their children.

On the first day of school, my teacher looked very mean. My first eye contact with him stirred in me a sense of fear. I felt he could see right through me, and I was not going to disobey his orders. He had a sharp bamboo stick to whip anyone who misbehaved. In our culture, a teacher was almost a divine being. He or she had a perfect right to discipline students in whatever way seemed fit and appropriate. My parents had total confidence in this man. He was the master of knowledge.

That day, I had to take a front-row seat with four other boys. The long tables were lined up facing the blackboard. *Lok kru* ("teacher" in Khmer) took down our names and tried to memorize our faces. All the children looked the same in their school uniforms—girls in their short blue skirts and boys in their shorts. The first lesson was to stand up to salute our flag. We stood outside singing the national anthem as the Cambodian flag was raised up the pole in the middle of the schoolyard. The breeze rippled the red-and-blue-colored strip of cloth with its white symbolic image of Angkor Wat in the middle, which represented our greatness and power as descendants of the Great Khmer Empire. There was excitement in it all, though I was nervous and afraid.

For the first few weeks, my teacher drilled the two components of the Khmer alphabet into our heads. He taught us by the rule of his stick. Anyone caught in the act of being a misbehaving boy was whipped with this stick. That was the way we learned the alphabet, through fear. I realized that school was not where I wanted to be. I thought it would be a fun place, where I could make a lot of friends. Every day, we were made to memorize, repeat, and write down each letter of the alphabet on the small blackboard we carried with us in our school bags. The first half hour of class was spent testing us to see how much we remembered. When the teacher called out a letter, we wrote it down on our blackboard and raised it up high for the teacher to see. We had to know our vowels and consonants and learn to put them together.

There were times when I didn't know how to write what was called out. Once I was busy trying to erase and rewrite what was being called out, and wasn't quick enough to raise my blackboard. The teacher walked toward me to check what I had written. He approached my desk and banged the stick on the table. Frightened, I jumped, raising my blackboard up high. He then pointed to my chalkboard for the whole class to see. Everyone was laughing and I didn't understand why. Then I realized that my blackboard was upside down. I had raised it too quickly, out of fear, and had my words upside down and incorrectly spelled. For that, my teacher asked me to extend my hand for the whip. I would not cry because I didn't want the other students to think I was weak. When I got home, I told Mother about it. I expected her to be protective of me, but she didn't seem to care. "Your teacher is like your second parent," she said. "He whipped you because he wanted you to pay more attention in class."

My school had children from the first to ninth grades. My brother Da was in the third grade when I was in the first. At the end of the day, we met up to walk home together. Our older brothers and sisters in high school in downtown Kampong Speu each rode their own bike to and from school. Da and I walked about ten to fifteen minutes, goofing around along the way. Da had become my favorite brother. I knew him better than any of my other brothers and sisters.

Sometimes at home, I felt as if I were still in school. Everyone had to be well-mannered and disciplined, although I could fool around more than the others because I was the youngest and everyone excused my fits and tantrums. My parents had established household rules for us, including respect and consideration for one another. At the dinner table we had to eat quietly and listen to our parents lecture us about family values, morality, and family status. When I was five, some of my older siblings were already in their mid-teens. My parents were very strict, especially with my sisters Mohm, Chan, and Theary, who were not allowed to go out dating or walking with boys. After eating, we had to study for a couple of hours before going to bed.

My third oldest brother, San, was assigned to tutor me each night before bedtime. He was every bit as tyrannical as my teacher. I was always afraid of him. He demanded that I be very alert and quick-minded and learn what he was trying to teach me. When I didn't respond quickly, he would strike me with a stick or bamboo switch. Every night, he force-fed knowledge into my brain. I had to memorize the alphabet, meticulously copy down every word, and repeat after him as he sounded out the words. My other brothers and sisters sat quietly doing their homework with great concentration, getting assistance from my father if they needed it. My father wanted to make sure we knew that education had gotten him far in life. That is why I had to endure San's impatient fits.

My oldest brother, Yean, was always the model student and finished second in his class at the university. During Lon Nol's reign, students rich and poor were sent to universities abroad to bring back needed skills and expertise so that they could help build Cambodia's economic, social, and political infrastructure. Yean was sent to Paris in 1971 on a government scholarship, and my parents were very grateful. "Look at your brother Yean," Father would always say. The government had given Yean two choices: study in France, or hold a high position in the national Marine Corps. It was a tough choice, since Yean loved the Marines, but my mother pressured him to accept the scholarship to study in France. Everybody thought he should go to France. It was every student's dream to study abroad. A few months after Yean decided to study in France, Khmer Rouge rockets would hit the Marine Corps' barracks along the Mekong River near the capital, and a few of his friends would be killed. It might easily have been him.

It was a big event when Yean came home from France in the summer of 1974 to visit. My parents took me along to greet him at the Pochentong International Airport. We arrived a few hours early. There were other people there with us to fill the airport with cheers and smiles. Many of them had never been outside of the country. To receive someone from far away made them feel as if they, too, could be arriving from and departing to faraway places.

We watched as the plane circled for a landing. A lady announced arrivals and departures in Khmer and French. Foreigners came . I was always afraid of them because they looked so big, so tall, so white and so blond, with blue eyes like Siamese cats. My whole family was anxious to see Yean arrive in his aristocratic clothes dabbed with French cologne. When he got off the plane, he greeted my parents, then picked me up and threw me into the air. Somehow, he looked different. His eyes even had a different glow.

My parents never thought about how France had changed their son. They were just happy to see him. The moment his eyes met hers, Mom started questioning him. "How are you, my son? Look at you. You are so thin. Didn't they feed you enough over there? Oh, you must have been eating too much Western food. Their food is not as filling as ours." She went on and on. I tried to get her attention, but had no success.

France, to me, was out there, somewhere beyond the rainbow. I'd love to have gone, too. Flying in an airplane was a dream of mine. Seeing real airplanes made my toy ones come alive. Sometimes in my dreams, I would climb into my model airplane and fly all over the world. There would be no particular destination. I'd just take off into the air and land whenever the dream ended.

Our country seemed so small compared to France or other places around the world. Europe must be very big, I thought. Yean told me all about it, but I was too young to grasp everything.

The best part of welcoming Yean was driving from the airport at night into Phnom Penh, where we would visit with relatives. The capital city was always so festive. Street lamps lit the roadways. There was so much to eat. People gathered at food stalls to eat and make chitchat. All varieties of fruit and fruit drinks were available. Men sold toys along the sidewalk to lure children into wanting things their parents couldn't afford. The last time Yean came home before the fall of Phnom Penh, airplane toys were all I wanted. When Mom said "no," Yean said, "yes," and he talked my mother into letting him buy some with his French money. But when the toy vendor wouldn't accept foreign money, I threw a tantrum. Mother would not spoil me, so she never fulfilled all my wishes. Instead, she spanked me a few times with her usual warning about tantrums; "If you're going to be like this, I will not take you anywhere again. You will have to stay with the rest of your brothers and sisters at home. Do you hear?"

Yean was always the super-nice brother. When Mother was harsh, he calmed me down with sweet promises. "Tomorrow I'll buy you the toy," he said. "Don't cry." Whenever I threw a fit, he'd pick me up and hold me tightly to his chest, rocking me to calm me down. Mom would shake her head with anger. My father wouldn't say a word. Sometimes his silence scared me.

Later in the afternoon on same day we had dessert at a street stall. But I was too exhausted from crying to even eat. When we got to our relative's house in Phnom Penh, Mother gave me a bath and put me right to sleep, nestled inside a mosquito net. That night was unbearably hot and humid. I couldn't sleep. The whole city was still awake with motorbikes and cars rattling on all night. Yean, out of politeness, stayed up with my parents to chat with our relatives. He probably didn't want to answer all those questions they were asking. The flight from France must have been very exhausting for him.

Before heading back to Kampong Speu, we stopped at the New Central Market as usual and bought lots of food. Mother planned to prepare a huge dinner, like we had at New Year to celebrate Yean's return. Yean was very grateful, because in France he could not get much Cambodian food. While he was home he devoured Mother's cooking. Every day, she cooked him something different.

As promised, Yean bought me the model airplane I'd wanted, as well as several toy cars. In the end, I always got what I wanted, more than my other brothers, and Da was particularly envious. We fought over everything. Only when one of my sisters threatened to take my toys away was I willing to share. When we arrived home, everyone except Da ran to hug Yean. Da came to search my bag to see what gift I'd received from him.

"Did you bring me anything from France?" asked Da. Everybody started to laugh.

"In fact, I did," Yean said. "I'll show you later after we eat, OK?" He'd brought everyone a small gift. Mom got some perfume. I got my airplane. That was all I cared about.

One day, several weeks before Yean was supposed to go back to France, my father came home from work and said to him, "You should leave right away. There has been unsettling news about our country." He said he had received many wounded people at the hospital. There was so much blood and not enough doctors and nurses to take care of the wounded. The soldiers brought tales of the Khmer Rouge attacking nearby villages, mostly at night.

Yean wanted to stay and spend time with the family, but because my parents felt so uneasy about it, he agreed. My mother packed his clothes, telling him through her tears not to worry. "You don't have to send money or anything to us. Just letters. That would make us more than happy."

My siblings carried Yean's luggage away. They looked very sad. I felt something awful was going to happen. My father's face seemed to say it was going to be a very long separation. I went along to the airport not understanding what our good-byes meant. After all, I was only five years old.

TWO

News & Rumors

Our life had already begun to change in 1970, when General Lon Nol, the defense minister who, supported by America, overthrew our king. We heard the jittering reports echoing through a transistor radio in our home. My father followed the news very closely during lunch, dinner, and in the evening. No one talked while the news was on. "What will happen to us if there's a war in our country?" my older siblings asked. There was no answer.

About four years later, when I was about six years old, I started noticing the worry on peoples' faces all the time. My father invited friends, family members, and neighbors to our house to listen to the news, especially *Voice of America,* and talk about it. My siblings used to fight over which radio stories they would to listen to. Insecurity and fear from the news reports gradually replaced the joy of soap operas, music, and folk stories.

I remember one night hearing the voices of demonstrators in the capital coming in loud and clear. When I asked what they were screaming about, Mother said that they were students loyal to the king and unhappy about the military police and the Lon Nol military government. My father saw this as a form of chaos that would bring Cambodia into a period of darkness and violence. He would not explain further. People everywhere said the Khmer Krahom were approaching.

"What are Khmer Krahom, Mother?" I asked.

"They are revolutionaries," she said. The word "revolutionaries" sounded strange. I knew that *krahom* meant red, so I thought maybe they were red-skinned Khmer, like the farmers who worked in the sun all day. (The Khmer Krahom would later become known by its French name, Khmer Rouge.)

Every day, I saw my parents and neighbors in front of our home talking about the events in the capital city. The radio said the Khmer Rouge were inching farther into the country and that Lon Nol's army, weakened by corruption and repeated defeats, could not hold them back any longer. Father said we were on the side of Lon Nol, who protected us from the Khmer Rouge. I knew then that they were bad people. The radio and rumors in the village also said that they were bad for our country.

Day by day, the war came closer to our village. I began to hear explosions not very far away. My parents were frightened. I was afraid, too, because I heard that the Khmer Rouge burned houses and temples, and killed anyone they caught.

Every evening after supper, Father gathered the family in the living room for the night. We slept on the floor downstairs so that we could escape, or run to the basement shelter, if the Khmer Rouge attacked. We turned the lights off before midnight, but Father kept a flashlight close by in case we needed to flee in the dark. All night long, we listened to the radio. Government soldiers and victims of the Khmer Rouge talked about blood and said the Khmer Rouge brutalized and killed the people they caught. They cut out their spleens to eat and hung body parts on trees. I never thought anyone could do such things, but it was no longer just a rumor. We began to believe that if the Lon Nol government lost the war, we would all die.

My second oldest brother, Lean, was supposed to leave for the United States in August,1975, but no one in the government would grant him an exit visa. Father wanted him to leave as soon as possible. Other wealthy people had already begun to send their families out of the country. Students who had gone abroad were warned not to return. The war was coming close to home and everyone was panicked and trying to find a way out. The Khmer Rouge were strong fighters and they were sure to take over Lon Nol's government soon.

I had so many questions. Who were the Khmer Rouge? What were they trying to do? Why were they so cruel? I didn't understand it, but I was told to fear them and expect the worst. I became afraid of playing in the backyard, although I sometimes hid in the rice field with Da and our friends. We wanted to see what the Khmer Rouge looked like. Were they really human? Were they really Khmer? Did they look like me? So much had been said about them, but we had not seen any.

One day, tanks began to roll over Highway 4 and soldiers in olive-green clothes arrived in town. They looked like ordinary government soldiers fighting to defend peace. Da and I followed them with the other children, cheering them on. It was like a circus, a parade of playing house and war in the rice fields. They waved as we waved, smiling assurances that they would bring peace to Cambodia again. There were so many soldiers that other activities along the road had to stop. People on motorcycles, oxcarts, cars, and bicycles froze to let the caravan of olive-green jeeps, tanks, and heavily armored trucks parade onward.

"Quick, quick, Seng! Come see the Khmer Rouge," Da said. I looked, but all I saw were ordinary soldiers in Lon Nol's uniforms. Neighbors and old people at the temple had said that the Khmer Rouge dressed in black, wore shoes made from car tires, and wrapped checkered *kramas,* or scarves, around their heads.

Then a truck rolled by with Khmer Rouge soldiers in it. They were all blindfolded, their hands bound behind their backs, and wore black uniforms. They were dirty and their uniforms were torn and stained with mud and sweat. Everyone was excited because it seemed that our soldiers were winning the war. Everybody, including my brothers and sisters, came to watch the victory parade. People cheered, waved, and screamed, "Hurrah, hurrah!"

Up close, however, the prisoners frightened me because of what I had heard on the radio, which made them out to be monsters. "Are they really Khmer Rouge?" I asked the other children. The color of their skin was not red. Their faces weren't any different from ours. Some were a little darker, and some had the same complexion as I did. How could they be so cruel? Maybe those stories were not true. I wondered what the Lon Nol soldiers would do to them now that they were prisoners. I ran to the garden behind the house where my mother was and told her what I had seen. "Mother, our soldiers captured some of the Khmer Rouge!"

It was a confusing situation for everyone, and all the reports were conflicting. The government radio said that the Khmer Rouge disguised themselves in civilian clothes to recruit others to join them. "Why would anyone want to join them if they're bad?" I wondered. Meanwhile, on their own radio station, the Khmer Rouge urged us to fight against American imperialism. "Americans will come dropping bombs in our country," they said. "America is a big and powerful country and will destroy us if we don't fight back." The exiled King Sihanouk, speaking now from the jungle, urged us to side with the Khmer Rouge because that was the only way to bring peace back to our country. The Lon Nol government painted the Khmer Rouge as evil people, while the king denounced the corrupt Lon Nol regime.

In the evening, older people gathered at the temple and my father talked about what the Khmer Rouge would do if they won the war. Some said they had come to save the people from the oppression of Lon Nol's government, to eliminate corruption, to support the poor, to bring King Sihanouk back, and to chase the Americans out of our country. But my father didn't think they were saviors. He doubted that the king had really joined the Khmer Rouge.

It seemed the entire country was spinning out of control. The families of many high-ranking officers had already left the country. Lower-ranking people had been left to their fates. The king was calling for everybody to join him in the jungle and I heard my father tell Mother that many farmers, students, and other followers had indeed left to join him. Everyone else was confused and afraid to go. My parents worried about what would happen to our family. Although they continued to smile and treat us as if nothing bad was happening, I could read the worry on their faces. A quiet suspense hung over us.

THREE

April 17, 1975 : Day of Betrayal

One calm night in April of 1975, at about two a.m., a rocket blast woke us all up with a start. We looked outside our windows and saw that a bomb had missed our house by only a few feet. The house next door was destroyed, and all the people in it were killed. Mother ran around frantically to see if we were OK. I was in my mother's arms screaming. My father looked right and left, eyes full of fear. Most of the radio stations from Phnom Penh were broadcasting that the Khmer Rouge had grown strong enough to take over the country. My parents thought the whole country was going mad. Father didn't know what to do, where to go, or how to protect us from the violence he anticipated. I heard him yell, "Everyone get downstairs, quick, quick!" My mother carried me while holding on to Da with her other hand. Then Father told us to get in the car and leave the house. The war had finally arrived at our doorstep.

The Khmer Rouge were attacking from all sides. Houses burned all around us. People fled on motorbikes, in cars, and in ox-carts down a narrow strip of Highway 4. Children were screaming.

Mother tried to hurry Father up. "Everybody is leaving," she said. But he was still wearing a sarong and had to put on pants. Everyone was panicking. "Where are the keys to the house?" my father asked. He couldn't find the key to the car, either. His pockets were empty.

"Maybe they're in your white shirt upstairs," said Mother.

"Come on, Father, let's go!" My brothers and sisters were frantic.

"Where are we going?" I asked, but no one answered me. Father ran upstairs and found the keys in his shirt pocket.

When we were finally in the car, another rocket flew past us and exploded. My mother started to chant her mantra to Buddha and called on her ancestral spirits to protect us. On the road, dead bodies were scattered about. Among them was a little boy I used to go to school with.

Beginning in January of 1975, the Khmer Rouge were attacking and came into our town at night to burn houses and kill people. Rockets were landing a few meters from where we ate and slept, and the sounds of gunfire were frequent.

We were afraid to stay at our home at night, so we stayed with friends in Kompong Speu, a few miles away, where it was more secure. Sometimes we returned to our home in daylight, when the Khmer Rouge had retreated to the jungle, to check on our house and feed our dog Akee who was guarding the house for us.

On one such visit, near sunset, Mother was trying to feed me when a rocket fell in our neighborhood. She dropped the spoon, grabbed me, and ran. She didn't know where she was taking me, but she was moving along with other people, trying to get to Father across town. Suddenly, rockets began to land all around us. Mother fell to the ground. I could barely hear myself screaming. I thought she had been hit by shrapnel or a bullet and had been killed. I saw other people getting hit and bodies were lying along the road. Blood was everywhere. Then my mother stood up and started running again, and I was hit in my right eye by shrapnel. My mother screamed in terror, thinking I had been seriously wounded. We found a house in which to hide with other people until the bombing stopped, and the sounds of war came to a halt for a while.

When it was fully dark, my mother headed towards downtown, carrying me on her hip, one hand pressed against my wound to stop the blood. People were walking toward the center of town with injured members of their families, looking for a hospital. My father was searching for us in his station wagon. When he finally found us and saw that I was bleeding, he drove us to his hospital, where he cleaned my eye and patched me up. Then he took us to his friend's house, where the rest of the family was waiting. We all slept together in the trench that the family had dug beside the house. I couldn't sleep because I kept having nightmares about the dead bodies I had seen on the road.

After that, government troops came, and every night, there was fighting between them and the Khmer Rouge. While I slept in her lap, I felt my mother tremble whenever the bombs fell. The war got louder and louder.

Meanwhile, people from the countryside continued to flee into the cities. The radio warned that Lon Nol's armed forces were losing the battle and that roads, bridges, telephone poles —virtually all means of transportation and communication — had been destroyed. Radio Phnom Penh said that the Khmer Rouge had advanced into Kampong Speu. My father and his friends said we were surrounded. Every night, the Khmer Rouge shot rockets into the city. Every morning when I awoke, I saw nothing but smoke and people crying over the loss of their parents, sisters, brothers, and children. My father's hospital filled up with wounded people, children and adults just lying there screaming for help.

Cambodia celebrates New Year for three days. Before dawn on April 14, 1975, the first day of Chaul Chnam Thmey, the Cambodian New Year, my mother woke me. She washed my face and dressed me in new clothes. My older sisters were already in the kitchen helping her prepare food. Usually she prepared a big New

Year feast for the family and relatives and would bring a great amount of food to the temple as offerings. But this year, there were only a few dishes to offer the ancestors and Mother did not go to the temple. Instead, she made the offerings in the house. I remember watching her, dressed in her traditional outfit, a silk sarong with her white lotus blouse, a hand-woven sash wrapped around her shoulders as she burned three incense sticks and lit candles to open our home to the angels and our ancestors. She prostrated herself before a Buddha statue to pray for peace and then poured wine for the ancestors and put different foods in a small bowl for them. Father had already left to see his patients and to get more medicines for the family.

Then, three days later, I heard my brother Reth outside, running and shouting, "No more war! No more war!" Da ran outside, too, and began cheering and shouting with Reth and some of the neighborhood children. The Khmer Rouge had arrived, waving white flags to proclaim peace. They wore black pants, shirts and caps, red-and-white checkered peasant scarves, *krama*, around their necks or heads. Hundreds of children were running after the soldiers. I ran after my brothers. We were so excited and curious to see what they looked like close-up and we cheered on their arrival. Many people came out of their houses, still wearing their nightclothes, wondering whether the news of peace was really true. There was cheering in the streets. Some children tried to hang on to the tanks as they rolled down the road.

It was a joyous New Year. I had never seen so many happy people, especially the children. The Khmer Rouge seemed to represent the end of war, which everyone had been praying for. Peace!

"We are here to save you!" proclaimed the soldiers.

I ran into the house to tell my mother the news. She was still in the kitchen, cooking food. "Mom, the Khmer Rouge say they are the good soldiers. They have brought peace. Hooray! We don't have to escape bombs and guns anymore. Peace has come, Mom! We can go home now," I told her. Mother was so happy to hear it.

She kissed me on the forehead but told me not to go outside alone.

Through the window, I saw people crowded around talking to their friends and neighbors about the war and the uncertainty of it all. I wanted to hear what they were saying.

"Where is your father?" Mother asked. "It's time for lunch. Could one of you go fetch him?" Just as San was about to leave, my father arrived, worry lining his face.

"Everyone, begin packing your clothes!" he said. My brothers and sisters had just been rejoicing over the coming of peace. Something was wrong. He was scaring us.

My mother didn't seem to worry. "Just calm down and eat. We don't have to pack right now," she said. "I can't see why we have to rush."

But my father knew what the Khmer Rouge soldiers were really up to. He had witnessed their bloodshed. He had heard stories from wounded soldiers, hundreds of them. Some had come to the hospital with shattered legs and arms, blown apart by shrapnel. "We cannot stay here!" Father screamed. "It's dangerous out there! Just do what I tell you. Start packing!"

He told my brothers and sisters to pack things into our four-wheel handcart, which could be pushed or pulled. We wouldn't be taking the car, he said. My mother started packing cooked and uncooked rice, some dried fish, plastic bags, a few cans of petrol, blankets, mosquito nets and a tarpaulin, pots and pans, plates and spoons—just enough for a few days. We made a last check around the house to see if we had forgotten anything. By the time we sat down for our meal, we'd lined up our luggage by the front door. We ate in silence.

FOUR

An Empty House

Just as we had finished eating, a second group of Khmer Rouge arrived. They, too, waved white flags of peace. But unlike the first group, they weren't smiling and friendly. Their guns were strapped to their shoulders in position to shoot and kill. They looked wild and mean. In actuality, the two groups were one. The first wave of Khmer Rouge had merely put on a happy mask at first to fool us. "We have come to save you all," a soldier announced over the loudspeaker. "Pack your things and leave as soon as possible. Don't take too much, because you're only going a few kilometers, and you'll come back in two or three days. The Americans are bombing. You must get out of here in three hours. Move and hurry!"

He fired his rifle into the air two or three times. People were frightened and started to rush their families out of the city. We were at our friends' house, where we'd been spending most of our time avoiding the violence. "We must make sure we stay together — stay put until I come back," Father said, as he ran out of the house to a hospital two blocks away to get medicines. Mother told San to rush out and buy more rice at a Chinese store.

When Father returned from the hospital, his face was full of fear. He had seen all the blood and bodies left behind from Khmer Rouge executions.

Then, like everyone else, we loaded our things onto the cart and left on the crowded, narrow road, in the heat of the day, not knowing where we would end up. Some people took more than they could carry. Some went with nothing but the clothes on their backs. Cars and motorbikes had slowed to a crawl. Some cars had been abandoned because there were so many people on the roads.

On the road, what we saw of the Khmer Rouge's atrocities made us move even faster. I watched as one man, a member of Lon Nol's army, was stripped of his hat and military uniform and made to kneel on the ground. He was then shot in the head. I yanked my mother's shirt, terrified. Any high-ranking officers caught were executed. No one associated with the Lon Nol government was spared.

The Khmer Rouge searched for people hiding in their homes. Anyone who refused to leave was shot immediately. Within two or three hours, the entire town was emptied.

We saw one rich Chinese man standing with his family outside their nice villa, watching the trail of evacuees. They clearly had no intention of leaving. Then two young Khmer Rouge, seventeen or eighteen years old, walked up to them and shot them, the whole family. They stripped them of their watches, gold, and diamonds — anything of value — and then pushed the bodies into a muddy swamp along the road. They couldn't drive the family's Mercedes, so they pushed it onto the side of the road as scrap metal. Then they set fire to the house.

We walked on, pretending not to see what we saw. In those few hours, we had seen nothing but death. My mother hid my sisters' gold necklaces, rings, bracelets, and ruby stones in her bundle, and hugged it close to her body.

My father told us to huddle closely into the moving, chaotic mass of humanity, as if to shield us from the dead bodies left along the way. People screamed, shed tears for mercy, and raised their hands toward the sky. Everywhere there was blood. It was unbearably hot and humid. I was shaking like a little mouse. My parents looked like beggars, Mother holding her bundle of clothes and Father dragging the handcart behind us while my brothers pushed. I clung to my mother as we hobbled along, not knowing when we would be allowed to return home.

The Khmer Rouge kept the crowds moving toward the countryside north of Kampong Speu. At a former Lon Nol army checkpoint, they put up a roadblock guarded by tanks Only a narrow path was left open, so narrow that only those who carried little or nothing could pass through. They then took from the people all motor vehicles, stereos, TVs, radios, cameras, cars, toys, wristwatches and jewelry; every large or valuable possession like mopeds, motorcycles, cars and trucks as they passed, and threw all of these possessions into the ditch by the side of the road along with a huge pile of weapons and Lon Nol army clothes.   What the rich fought for all their lives had become pieces of trash. The Khmer Rouge would mock these objects by wearing, for instance, two or three watches around their wrists. They listened to a transistor radio close to their ears. They jumped up and down on top of cars like monkeys. They crashed cars into the mud of the rice fields. People who refused to give up their cars or other possessions had their car keys shoved down their throats or were forced to eat dirt like pigs.

The Khmer Rouge would have been treated as backward peasants, as children from the jungle who had never known city life, except for one thing; they had guns. Most of the Khmer Rouge soldiers were nothing but children themselves.

As we climbed up a curving slope past the checkpoint, I took a glimpse back to say good-bye to Kampong Speu. I had never seen so many people before, all moving en masse. It was difficult to walk among them because they were all carrying something and competing for space, too—especially those with bikes and oxen carts who were allowed to pass the checkpoint because those were used by farmers. My mother never let go of me. I held on to her sweaty hand, squeezing it tightly. Some children, separated from their parents, were seen crying along the roadside. I remember seeing one handicapped boy who was all alone, crying under a tree. When I saw him, I jerked my mother's hand to make her look. Her face was drained and sad. Her already-light complexion became more pale. She had never walked so far from her house and her kitchen.

"Keep walking close to Mother," she told me. "I don't want to ever lose you."

It felt like we had been walking for days. Everyone's face was red and our shirts were soaked through from the hot April sun. Every ten or fifteen minutes we craved water. My father told us to stop and rest for a while and Mother unrolled a straw mat beneath a shady tree for us to sit on. We couldn't keep moving any longer. There were other people resting as well. No Khmer Rouge saw us.

"How much farther do we have to go from the city?" Da asked.

I was curious, too, but no one seemed to know the answer. My parents didn't show any sign of hope that we would ever return. There was a longer road ahead, but first, we had to eat. It had gotten a little cooler. My sister unpacked the rice and dried fish we had brought from home. I started to salivate the moment I smelled the food. But just as she was getting things ready, a Khmer Rouge came up to us and told us to keep moving.

"We didn't tell you to stop," he said. "Keep moving! We will tell you when to stop!" We didn't dare protest. His AK-47 was enough to make us pack up again and start moving again. We had to eat while we walked, shoveling a handful of rice at a time into our mouths.

That was the first time any of us had ever walked so far. I was so tired. I couldn't walk anymore, and Father had to put me on the cart. There was no city ahead, only the vast country plain, stretching far beyond what my eyes could see. Rice fields filled the landscape. Small thatched huts were built between palm trees. I had never seen anything like it.

Finally, as the sun sank, some breezes blew our way. My brother Da was crying for rest, food, and water. I looked at my family and saw how tired they all were. None of us knew when we would be able to stop. Across a bridge, we saw people resting, so we decided to do the same. My father found a spot close to other people. We put down our baggage and spread our straw mat on the ground. The sun went down and left us homeless in the middle of nowhere. For a moment, everything seemed so quiet and still.

My father and my brothers San and Reth left to gather some firewood and water for Mother to cook with. My older sisters collected some hay and dead branches to start the fire. Mother had never cooked outside or without a stove before. But she figured out how to make a cooking tripod with rocks. My brothers and father came back with plenty of water and firewood for the night. We all sat in a circle next to the fire waiting for Mother to serve us rice one at a time. She handed me a small bowl of rice mixed with soup and dry beef. Everything we ate tasted so good. It was the best supper I ever had, despite there being so much sadness in it.

Everyone around us was in the same situation, in their family circles, dreaming of the day when things would go back to normal again. We were all thinking the same thing, that maybe in a few more days we would be allowed to go back home again.

It grew late, and my mother arranged space for us to sleep. "It will be a very long day ahead of us," she said. "Let's sleep for strength." At first, I thought it was fun, seeing hundreds of people sleeping everywhere in the rice field as if they were on a camping trip. The sky was full of stars. I lay beneath them imagining flying on an airplane somewhere, maybe to visit Yean in France. My father had always thought that I would become a pilot since I liked model airplanes so much. He told me that one day when I grew up, he would send me to France to study aviation and follow in Yean's pursuit of a Western education. Now I doubted that I would ever be able to go to France. I wondered if Yean knew what was happening to us. Up above, heavenly sparks took the shape of a kite. I fell asleep capturing their brightness in my memory. Even now, wherever life takes me, I remember the stars that night.

My father joined a group of men near us; the fear on their faces was a premonition. I did not understand what they were talking about. All I remember was that after talking with the other men my father warned us to always keep silent and never tell any of the Khmer Rouge about our past if they asked us. "Just say that we were poor city people," he said. He had correctly surmised that anyone tied to the grandeur of the past would be killed. Soldiers, doctors, bourgeoisie, teachers, and government officials would be mercilessly murdered. That is what each of those men was afraid of—one day, they might be discovered.

In the middle of the night, while everyone slept, I woke from a quiet dream to the silence around me. For a moment, I thought everyone had left and I was all alone, like the handicapped boy who had lost his family and had been left under a tree crying. Then I was startled by someone's coughing. I heard babies crying and people whispering from a distance. I saw that my mother was right next to me, using her hand as a pillow. The stars were still there, but the morning light was about to chase them away. I fell back to sleep again and began to dream: *Yean's plane was shot down while it was getting ready to land. The sky was empty of planes arriving and departing. Cambodia had no birds to see, no flowers for the bees. The whole country was empty of people. My parents, sisters, and brothers were all gone. I was left all by myself in the fog to open my eyes to the sun.*

Suddenly, I heard the Khmer Rouge drive past us in their trucks and olive green jeeps on their way back to Kampong Speu. Nobody could go back to sleep after that. Mohm and Chan, my sisters, with my mother started a fire to cook rice for breakfast. It was a little chilly. I grabbed my sisters' blankets to cover myself and fell back to sleep. It was around six in the morning, when the sun was about to rise, that my mother woke me up again.

"It's time to get up, my little boy," she said.

"Where are we going so early, Mother?" My eyes opened to a murkiness that was all around me. It felt as if I was still dreaming.

"We have to get moving soon," my mother said.

"I don't think I can walk again, Mother."

"Let me wash your face."

Mother poured cold water from a small pail onto her palm to pat over my face. That woke me up and opened my eyes to a bright new day. We didn't know when we would be able to stop again so she made us all a full breakfast of rice and salted meat. The meat had a delicious aroma as she grilled it over the fire. My brothers couldn't wait for it to be done cooking.

Soon after we ate, we saw people already up and on the move, walking past us. The Khmer Rouge must have told them to move on. We rolled up our mat and blankets and packed up our cooking supplies. Mother had made us some food for the road in case we got hungry.

The sun was glaringly bright. It was going to be another hot day. On the road, our small clan became a part of the moving mass again. Noises competed for everyone's attention. Children screamed. Cows bellowed. Pots and pans clanged. Old men spat to clear their throats. On both sides of the road, dead bodies were scattered about, rotting and stinking. We guessed they must have been the bodies of Lon Nol soldiers killed by the Khmer Rouge before they took over our town. Some bodies had come floating up to the surface in the middle of a rice field. My mother didn't want me to see the blood, but while we were walking, I was taking everything in. The ones who had fallen sick were left to die on the way. No one was able to help anyone else.

It had been more than four days since we'd left Kampong Speu and we were still on the road without a destination. My family decided to break away from Highway 4 and clandestinely took a path down a winding road toward a small village hidden in the jungle. We came upon an empty house and stayed for a while. My parents looked for signs of life, but the whole village was empty. The Buddhist temple was emptied of monks and nuns. Then, out of nowhere, villagers approached us with rice and meat to trade for gold and watches. I was amazed. We had almost run out of rice. But my mother still had her little purse filled with treasures. One Chinese man had a bag of money with which to buy rice, but the villagers only accepted gold or diamonds, so he had to return to his family with the worthless paper currency. My mother, on the other hand, came back to us with enough rice and meat to feed us for a few more days.

We walked some more and came to another abandoned village, where we thought we could settle. After a few minutes' search, Father found a small empty thatched house for us to live in. This house had a look of sadness, surrounded by weeds and cobwebs. I wondered if our house in Kampong Speu would become like this, old and ragged without the sound of people coming and going.

"Are we going to stay here now?" I asked my mother.

She was too exhausted to answer. She was just happy to rest after our very long walk. My brothers and sisters began to clear the bushes and clean the house to make it livable again. Other city people who were being evacuated like us started to arrive as well. There were no traces of Khmer Rouge soldiers directing us where to go. They had told us to keep walking, but we didn't understand where to go. "You will come back in a few days," they had told us. Yet a few days had already passed and no one had come to us and said, "You all can go back home now." I kept wondering whether we would ever see our home again.

The first thing Mother did was to look around for any sign of a garden with fruit and vegetables. She and my sisters found edible flowers and some vegetables, left to become wild. She also found some sweet potatoes that the villagers had planted but never had the chance to harvest. That evening, she cooked us a good dinner, with boiled sweet potatoes for our dessert. A friend of my father's named Both Tha, who worked at the same hospital and had found himself in the same group of people as we were in, joined us.

Later that night, I heard distant wolves howl back and forth to one another. I thought of how tigers might prowl around this jungle, how they might attack and eat humans. When I asked my mother if there were any tigers nearby, my sister got angry and smacked me on my thigh. "You don't ask that kind of question here," she said. "While we are in a strange place like this, you should never talk about wild animals. It's bad luck." The ancestors, she said, can get angry and send the wild animals after us. She said that we should pray instead for the spirit of the jungle to guide and help us.

In the morning, Mother got up early to clean the house and organize our lives around our new home. My father was fixing our handcart while Both Tha cleared the weeds and grass near the house. Then we saw a group of Khmer Rouge soldiers on an ox-cart. The sound of their whip drove the oxen down the road. They had come to chase us out again.

"Who told you to settle here?" they asked.

My father told them that we followed what other people were doing. "When we saw others begin to settle here, we decided to find a place to settle as well."

"Hey, *Met*! Get your family together and leave this house at once!" ordered one of the Khmer Rouge soldiers. (They required us now to address one another as *met*. I had never heard the word before. In Khmer, *met* means "comrade.") "This house does not belong to you, nor does it belong to us. It belongs to Angkar and you are not allowed to stay. Be out of this house by noon."

"Where are we supposed to go, sir?" Both Tha asked.

"*Met*, from now on you must not address me or anyone else as 'sir,'" one of them said. "That is the bourgeois language. Angkar will not tolerate city language."

We stood looking at one another with sadness, not knowing where we were heading. The Khmer Rouge instructed us to leave, but yet again didn't tell us where to go. We gathered our things again. Mother had hoped we could make this house our home since there was a good place to make a garden. Yet we could not question the Khmer Rouge. We had to obey because we never knew what would happen to us if we didn't. The journey took us deeper and deeper into the forest, until another Khmer Rouge soldier appeared and finally told us where to settle.

FIVE

The Jungle Cries Out

Sangkear Village was in the thick of the jungle and mountains, although it was only about fifty miles from downtown Kampong Speu. None of my family had ever traveled this far into the jungle. The native people were Khmer, like us, but had lived all their lives in this remote area. They spoke to us with such heavy accents that we could hardly understand them. Most of the children were dark-skinned and unkempt, and stood in front of their stilt homes staring at us strangers. I wondered how they got food, toys, and access to the city. There were no cars, motorcycles, markets, or schools. They used oxcarts for transportation and the only road in the village was a narrow dirt path made by their two-wheeled carts. It looked like train tracks cut through grass. At night it was so dark. We were terrified of the scorpions and other creatures that came crawling near us. When my sisters screamed in fright, the Khmer Rouge laughed at us. We had never experienced the deep jungle and we were very worried about getting lost.

The Khmer Rouge referred to us as the New People and the

villagers as the Old People. Some of them had been part of the revolutionary movement from the start and were assigned to teach and indoctrinate us in "the way of Angkar." *Angkar* means "the organization." Under Angkar, all people would start anew and live as equals, which is why they had moved us out of the city. There would be no rich and no poor.

But in the villagers' eyes, we were not equals. We were city people, reeking of wealth and leisure. They seemed to hate us and to look upon us as if we had never worked for anything. They thought we'd always had it easy, that we'd fulfilled our every desire. Therefore it was necessary to train and reeducate us so that we could live like them, plowing the fields day by day, laboring to fill our stomachs.

Maybe they were right. I'd always gotten whatever I wanted. We lived in a very nice house. I had fine clothes for every occasion. I didn't have to worry about anything because my parents took care of everything. They even had savings so that I could study abroad when I got older. I would have had it made if the war hadn't come. But my father worked hard for our food, sometimes staying at the hospital late into the night taking care of his patients, and disappearing so early every morning that I hardly got to see him. Nothing was as easy as people thought.

At the beginning, some of the Old People were very helpful. When we arrived at the village, it was mostly jungle, with only a small village. Then suddenly hundreds of New People families were there, settling down and trying to survive. The village leader gave every family an equal piece of land to clear so that we could build our own homes and grow our own food. Since my father had no experience building a house, a Khmer Rouge family helped us build ours. They showed us how to gather straw, bamboo, and wood for a hut on stilts—we all helped clear the land and gather the materials. Although it was nothing like our house in Kampong Speu, it kept us out of the rain. It had a roof of palm leaves and a floor of bamboo slats. I remember how my mother smiled when it was done. All of the huts were built in a row in the same size and style. We all slept together in one room, lying on our straw mat on the rough floor. No more soft mattresses and pillows. For light we lit a piece of a rubber tire. It looked like this was to be our new home, and so it was for almost three months.

Until we could grow our own food, the Khmer Rouge distributed food from their stores. Of course, my parents didn't know how to cultivate rice, so the family who had helped us build the house showed them how. This was to be our new life. Suddenly, we were subsistence farmers and gathered food from our natural environment. In Kampong Speu, we would go to the market almost every day and buy everything we needed. Now, we had to grow and find everything ourselves.

We were all assigned work. Two of my brothers and all three of my sisters were taken away to cut wood and clear vines outside the village. None of them had ever done hard, menial work before. My brothers had spent their time studying and my sisters had helped with the housework. Now everyone was working the land. Under the stress of this kind of work in harsh jungle conditions, some of the New People began to get sick with malaria and die.

Still, our new, quiet, peasant life had its positive side. My brothers and sisters were allowed to come back from work to have lunch with the rest of the family. We weren't hungry. We weren't idle. My other brothers helped my parents plow the field on the land given to us.

Like the children of some of the Khmer Rouge families, I was given a job herding cattle. Every day, we would wake up early and take the cows into the fields of grass. While they were feeding, I would go around collecting mushrooms and wild vegetables for my mother.

A village boy, Khoeun, and I became good friends. We often took our cattle into the fields together. He taught me how to climb trees, find wild nuts, hunt animals, and catch fish. He knew his way around the jungle. He had never been in the city and had never seen cars or electricity. When I told him I had a lot of toys at home in Kampong Speu—airplanes, cars, and tanks—he asked what an airplane was. I drew a picture on a sandy spot with a stick and told him it was a machine that could fly up in the air. I told him it needs a runway for taking off and landing. He was fascinated. I showed him how to make an airplane out of banana-tree bark and he showed me how to make oxen and other animal figurines out of clay.

Among the herders, Khoeun was my best friend. I admired him because he wasn't afraid of going into deep, unfamiliar, mosquito-infested jungle areas. We went fishing, too. One time, we had so much fun catching fish that we forgot all about our cows. At the end of the day, we counted the cows and realized that one was missing. We had to go look for it. We got lost for several hours looking for the missing cow. I was so frightened that we'd be attacked by tigers, but Khoeun, who was always brave, didn't seem to worry. The sun was about to set and we were in the middle of nowhere. I started shouting for someone to help us, but no one seemed to be around.

Khoeun pretended not to hear me. He kept walking, looking for the cow as if he were the master of the forest. We found a wild water buffalo getting up from bathing in a small, muddy pond. I wanted to run because it looked as if it was ready to charge toward us, but Khoeun didn't budge. He stared straight into the wild beast's eyes until it surrendered and retreated. The sun was about to sink away, but Khoeun kept going until the lost cow was found. We heard its bell clinking in the distance. Khoeun's sharp ears could hear it from miles away. He climbed a tree to see where it might be. Then, after we'd caught it, we had to figure out a way to get back to our village. An old man who was herding his cows pointed us to a trail less than a mile from where we were.

By the time we got back home, my parents were worried sick. "Where did you go?" Mother asked me. "The other children didn't know where you were. All the cows were here, but we didn't see you. I was so worried that something had happened to you."

"Mother, we had to take our cows to a different place," I told her. "One of them got lost so we had to go find it. Khoeun took me deep into the forest. We got lost for a while, but we found the cow and our way back home."

"You shouldn't go to places you don't know," my brothers and sisters chimed in. "If you had gotten killed, we wouldn't know where to look for you."

I remember how everyone had waited for me. None of them had eaten dinner yet and it was getting dark, but Mother took me to the back of the hut and gave me a bath. They all waited patiently, although they were a bit irritated and angry.

My friendship with Khoeun was eventually cut short. One day, we went far from the village. He went one way and I went another, foraging for wild food. I was more interested in mushrooms, but Khoeun liked to climb trees to take the eggs from birds' nests. That day, he came upon something unusual: a nest full of eggs in a low shrub. He was putting them in his shirt's pockets when he heard something rattling, moving through the long, dry grass. It was a snake. When he saw it, he started to run. The snake slithered after him to reclaim her eggs. Khoeun was too slow. It zigzagged faster than his short little legs could carry him and when it caught up to him, it bit him on the arm. He fell, but he dropped some eggs to stop the snake from devouring him. The bite was painful and he went home crying. The other children tried to help by tying his arm with a *krama* to keep the poison from spreading.

When I got home, I heard him crying. His parents took him to a traditional healer, but the healer couldn't help him. Khoeun's father knew that my father knew a lot of medicine and he brought Khoeun to him for help—but my father hadn't brought along any anti venom medicine. He gave Khoeun intravenous glucose, but it didn't stop the poison, which had already spread. His body was swollen and his skin had turned a pale blue. A couple of days later, Khoeun died.

Khoeun's family laid his body on a bamboo bed and wrapped it in a blanket. I stood outside of his hut thinking of him, my good friend. I wished my father had had all the right medicine to save his life. He was the only Khmer Rouge friend I had. My best friend. I knew I would miss him and feel lonely when I went back to the forest to take care of cows and water buffaloes.

Still, that was my only real sadness for almost three months. We adjusted very well to life in the village. We had enough to eat. The Khmer Rouge leader was kind. We had become like the peasants, living day by day, laboring to bring our food home. Though it was not the same as our home in Kampong Speu, my parents didn't complain.

Then the village leader was replaced, and everything began to change. One evening, two Khmer Rouge soldiers wearing Maoist Chinese caps came to inform us of a decree by the new leader. Their presence demanded fear and respect. They had wrapped *kramas* around their necks to identify themselves with the struggles of peasants and they carried AK-47 rifles. My parents thought perhaps they were bringing us good news, that we were allowed to go home. Instead, the soldiers said the new leader was calling every adult to attend a required meeting. Everybody had to go, even the old leader who had been so kind to us.

Maybe the meeting is to inform people that we can leave soon and return home because the war is over, I thought. It would be so nice to see my house and my dogs again. Akee was perhaps dead. Last time we saw him, he was skinny, and sad that we'd left him all alone in the house. Everything in our house was perhaps gone. Nothing might remain but the ashes of a burned-down house, village, and town—a city emptied of people. Still, how joyful it would be, even if we had to build our lives all over again, to stay on our land and live in peace.

On the other hand, I thought, what if Angkar had called all the adults to this meeting to be killed? What would we do without our parents? We had heard that the new village leader was ferocious, but nobody had met him. No one knew who he was. We hoped that he wouldn't kill people and make us do horrible things. My sisters and brothers and I couldn't sleep. All of us sat around our burning piece of rubber, waiting for our parents to return. Each of us was consumed with worry. When we saw that some of our neighbors had returned, we got even more scared. We asked people if they had seen our parents. One of the women told us that they were coming. We were so happy to see them when they finally got home.

"Mother, Father!" we exclaimed, jumping up to hug them. "Will we be able to go home soon?"

"I am sorry, dear children," my mother replied. "I'm afraid that we can't return home, not just yet. We must gather our belongings and get ready to leave this village. They are taking us to another place." I remembered my mother's drooping eyes, which displayed almost no hope. They were told that we were supposed to walk to the highway the next morning and wait for a truck to take us somewhere.

We woke up in the fog. Mist clouded the forest and it looked like rain. It seemed to be a bad omen. Everything had changed so quickly. The neighbors came to say good-bye. My father's friend Both Tha said our families should leave together. But we hadn't gotten our things ready yet, so my father told him to go ahead without us. After we had gathered everything, we went to Khoeun's family to say good-bye and they gave us some rice for the road.

It took a whole day to make it to the highway. I didn't know where I was. I only knew that there was forest all around. It was raining harder and harder, and we didn't have anything to cover us. When we got to the highway, we were soaked. It was very cold. Then the rain stopped and the sky began to clear. The moon looked over us and cried. Hundreds of families were being evacuated on this dusty red road. My brothers and sisters were carrying things and pulling a handcart, and I was holding on to my mother's hand, and asking her where they were taking us. "I don't know, my dear. Don't ask. Just keep walking."

That night, Mother unfolded her mat on the field for us. She went to sleep thinking of my brother in France. All choked up and scarcely believing what was happening to us, she to tried to offer up all her tears and suffering under the new regime as a sacrifice so that Yean wouldn't return. It was a good clear night, but it was so sad. There we were, surrounded by strangers, sleeping in an open field waiting to be picked up by the phantom trucks.

The next morning, our bodies were soaked with mist and dew. Finally, the trucks came. We piled into one truck like cattle. A few hours later, we were at a train station. Like animals, we were packed into a train bound for Battambang in the west. It was hot and congested, with all the sweat and smells of people. The sound of the steam train became a haunting sound in my dreams. I cried nonstop.

The trip took three days, but there was no food, no basic necessities. People hadn't eaten anything for days. Some people got sick and died in the train car. My sisters and brothers stood craning their necks into the corridor for air. The soldiers who were riding on top of the train occasionally allowed some of the passengers to sit with them. I fell asleep on my mother's lap in hunger and thirst.

After three days, we reached the Pursat Province station, where we were all unloaded. We were told we would need to wait several days before moving on to our next destination, but no one told us what to do or where to go. There were many other families who had arrived here before us who had created shelters along the dikes. We were surrounded by rice fields. We were incredibly thirsty, but the water in the rice field was filled with leeches, so we had to use mosquito netting to strain the water for drinking. We weren't given any instructions about what to do. On that day of the monsoon season, the dark clouds moved in and suddenly the rain was pouring down on us and we were soaking and wet. There were many other families who arrived here before us who had fashioned shelters along the dikes. There was nothing nearby but a rice field. People were sleeping on the dykes and roads around the flooded field, sometimes on top of each other because there was so little room. They didn't have anything to protect themselves from the rain. My family had a plastic tarp for cover, but the heavy rain still got to us. Our mat was saturated with water. We slept with our clothes wet. There was no wood to start a fire for cooking. Everything was scarce. I noticed there were many Cambodian-Chinese families around us, hobbling and crying because they didn't know what to do. They were so used to the leisurely life of the city that they couldn't take the degradation. Whenever the Khmer Rouge walked by, they would become silent. The Khmer Rouge would come and take whatever they wanted from them, telling them that Angkar wanted this and that. The Chinese had no choice but to give it to them.

One of my sisters and I went around gathering scraps of wood and leaves for a fire. We noticed that some people had hanged themselves in the trees because they couldn't take it anymore. Their dead bodies hung like some strange fruit from poisoned trees. I can still see them in my sleep.

We still had a bit of food left from the village, and Mother rationed the food among us so that what we had would last longer. We ate what we had little by little. All I did was cry. It was hard to sleep because the ground was wet. Everywhere you went there were dead bodies. When my mother walked off to go to the bathroom behind bushes, she saw many bodies left unburied to rot and for vultures to feast on.

It was like the hell they described in Buddhist scripture. In our temples, hell is often depicted in vivid wall paintings of people with fangs and cut-up faces begging for forgiveness. Those who have wronged others in their previous lives have their bellies cut open. Hundreds huddle in desperation for food and some are burned and stewed in hell's cooking pot. Their souls will be trapped forever in a cycle of madness. They will never be reborn. It seemed somehow as if my family and I had been kidnapped by Khmer Rouge demons and taken into this hell.

My family had been one of the strongest. We had already survived months of suffering, but I'm sure we would have died there in Pursat if a train hadn't come to take us elsewhere. Once again, we huddled inside a boxcar, fighting for space and air. We were being transported to Battambang in the northwest section of Cambodia, where the largest rice plantations in the country were located. Whoever didn't catch the train was left to die.

It took one night and a day to reach our new destination. I remember the woman next to me accidentally spilled a chemical that smelled like vinegar on my left foot. It was so hot and stinging that I yelled for my mother's help. My foot was burning and the crowd was choking from the strong smell. My father quickly washed my leg with water and wrapped it with his small *krama*. I was in tears and lay down against our bundles to rest for several long hours. I thought I was not going to live to see our new destination. But when I woke up, we were in Battambang Province, being unloaded. That night, we slept at the train station.

We still didn't know where we were going. "When are we going to get there?" I asked many times. My tired brothers and sisters were moaning and groaning, not only about the trip but about the uncertainty. "Don't complain!" my father ordered, afraid that the Khmer Rouge would hear them leave all of us by the roadside or take us away to a mass grave.

From the station in Battambang, we were loaded onto army transport vehicles with thousands of others, mostly middle-class families from cities who had never set foot outside of the marketplace, and sent to Svay Sisophon, a city to the west, near the Thai border. From there, we were led to Tuk Chjo, a village of nothing but rice fields. There we'd stay for the four years of the Khmer Rouge rule.

SIX

Village of a Thousand Sorrows

We had been dropped off on the highway between Siem Reap and Battambang Provinces in Svay Sisophon, a place that seemed hostile and uninhabitable. In Kampong Speu, we'd had many trees and could see mountains in the distance. Here, we saw nothing but flat fields flooded with water and a river that seemed to go on forever. Except for a bridge that arched over the river, there was only water. It was as though we had been dumped on the shore of an ocean. Hundreds of us abandoned on this windy plain of water huddled to keep warm.

"There's a village ahead, up that way," someone shouted. "Move toward it! It's called Tuk Chjo and it's your new home." That sounded permanent.

We were herded toward the fields. The Khmer Rouge wanted us to cultivate rice on this flooded plain even though the water was too deep to cultivate anything. We walked to the nearly empty village of Tuk Chjo along a broken, muddy road. I could see a few palm trees in other distant villages. When we got to our destination, we were told to wait for a village leader to assign us houses. The dry land looked like a small island in the middle of the ocean. I was wet and hungry. We couldn't cook anything, but my mother retrieved from her bag the leftover salted rice she had saved and gave a little to each of us. My father and older siblings went to relieve themselves and returned with dry wood and branches for a fire. We waited many hours, from morning to late in the evening, before the village leader finally came with a group of soldiers and told us where to go.

"Attention!" he said. "You New People"—again we were called New People, those of us who never had officially joined their revolution—"must stay here tonight. Tomorrow we will assign you by family to a section in the village where you will stay. Angkar has sent you under my command. This is District Five. Do as Angkar tells you." We still didn't know who Angkar was, but nevertheless felt we had to obey everything. All of us who had been unloaded from the trucks were now crowded together on this little island for the night.

My parents laid down the straw mat on a dry spot. I dozed off while my older siblings helped Mother to set up mosquito nets and tried to make a fire. Other people were doing the same thing. We all wondered why we had been brought here, so far from home. It was wet, cold, and windy, and the ground was soggy. When my mother woke me up to eat, it was very late into the night. We ate in silence. Out there, in the middle of nowhere, other people were sleeping and eating. They burned cut-up tires to light their family circles and the flames made it seem as if we were floating, lost, on a raft, drifting with the slow-moving currents. My parents started to cry. It had all happened so fast. One day we were well off; the next day, we were dirt poor and homeless.

My father understood this. Again he warned us, whispering quietly, "No one say anything to anyone about our family, about our past, our family history. Nothing. Just pretend that we were poor. Tell them that we collected cans and junk for a living."

Before our forced evacuation, my father had seen with his own eyes how the Khmer Rouge killed wealthy, bourgeois, and educated people because they were corrupted and exploited the peasants. . He knew that anyone with credentials, anyone who had worked as a government official, teacher, doctor, or lawyer, would be killed as subversives—Angkar wanted to make everyone equal in socioeconomic status by eliminating the rich and educated. Father had heard about their tactics, and how they would try to trick us. At that moment, I felt my fate change. A hole was punctured inside me for these people to fill with lies. All of us now had to lie to survive. If we were honest about the past, the Khmer Rouge would kill us.

After midnight, the wind calmed down. Everyone else was asleep, exhausted by the long journey. In the darkness, I heard people coughing, babies crying, crickets and other insects chirping. I couldn't sleep. My stomach was growling and I had diarrhea. I woke my mother to take me out for a squat, but my father took me instead. He didn't want to go too far because Khmer Rouge soldiers might think we were trying to run away.

"Father, I can't hold it any longer," I told him. Father took off my pants and let me relieve myself right where we stood, even though it was close to all the people. Then he washed me up in the river and brought me back to our place. Mother forced an anti-diarrhea pill down my throat and rubbed my tummy with Tiger Balm to keep me from vomiting. I felt nauseated, but my mother's love put me right to sleep, with no worry on my mind, as if it all had been a dream. In my sleep I wasn't aware that anything bad was happening to us. I dreamed that everything was normal again. *I was back in my home in Kampong Speu with all my family. In the morning, I would be going to the bazaar with my mother. The smell of fresh fruit, vegetables, and raw meat wove together. I was running and playing with my friends out behind my house.*

"Get up, my son, have some rice porridge while it's still hot." I hadn't heard the cock crowing, and my mother's voice woke me.

"I'm not hungry, Mother. I'm still tired. I want to sleep."

"It's morning. Everybody is already up. Have some rice porridge."

Our rice was running out, so Mother had only put a fistful in the pan, and we didn't have any salted fish to make it tasty, so the porridge tasted like water. My brothers drank it from their bowls.

"Mother, look there!" I said, pointing. The Khmer Rouge were coming like crows and ravens, all black with their red beaks pecking into our fearful hearts. Their dark eyes pierced us.

"We are now ready to put you into groups," announced one of the Khmer Rouge, a tall, scrawny peasant. We weren't allowed to choose where we would stay. These soldiers took groups of two or three families and crowded us into tiny thatched houses. Our group of more than twenty people was given a thatched house on stilts with a tin roof. We hardly had any room to move around in or sleep. Every family stayed to itself, squeezing between the strangers. Those who tied hammocks between the posts outside were told to take them down because it wouldn't be fair to those who didn't have hammocks. They wanted us all inside no matter how tight the space was. More people were still on their way. Some were taken farther out to other villages.

One night, the village leader came to inform us all of a meeting. Every family member must attend, he said, young and old. We would be told about Angkar's plan for our lives. We now belonged to Angkar. There are no rich or poor. Angkar had eliminated all the imperialism and classicism. We will all wear the same clothes, eat the same food and work in the same fields. Angkar had fought many years for us, and we must build our new lives with Angkar. If anyone talks about their old lives, Angkar will take you away for reeducation. At that meeting, we were told that those who had Chinese, Cham (Muslim), or Vietnamese ancestry would be allowed to return to their homelands. Those who had been soldiers of the previous government would be taken to Phnom Penh to work—"Angkar needs soldiers at all levels to help fight the imperialist Americans," the village leader said. He then appealed to former professors, students, teachers, and doctors to serve Angkar, too—

"Angkar needs people with education to help rebuild our country as soon as possible." He spoke into a megaphone so that everyone could hear. People in black clothes were shouting, *"Che yo! Che yo! Glory to Angkar! Glory to Angkar!"*

Many people stood up to volunteer, believing that the Khmer Rouge were sincere, and admitted their past.

"Let us appreciate these brave individuals who have stood up," the soldier with the megaphone shouted. *"Che yo! Che yo!"* everyone shouted. Even Father raised his hand in a cheer. But he knew what they were saying was a hoax and he and my mother sat still, with us huddled all around them.

"Don't anyone stand up," whispered my Father.

"Listen to your father," Mother whispered to us.

"Write down your name on this piece of paper," the leader told those who had stood up. "You are Angkar's special comrades. You will set an example for others." Some people with Chinese, Cham, or Vietnamese ancestry were excited at the prospect of returning home. But my father knew something was not right. He could smell blood, and knew that these people were signing away their lives. They weren't going home. They were on their way to a mass grave.

I wondered, If the Khmer Rouge are that kind and generous, why are they letting only the Vietnamese, the Chams, and the Chinese go home? Why not everybody? Something is wrong.

Two days later, the "special comrades" were told to wait for the trucks along the riverbank. Some said good-bye to their friends and neighbors. I was sitting on the front steps of our new house watching two of the families who had been living with us get ready to leave. They were so happy to be returning home. In the afternoon, two or three trucks took them away. My father knew that these people were on their way to interrogation and execution.

The Khmer Rouge continued to lay down their rules and regulations. The village leader told us we must attend education meetings every night. At first he didn't seem mean, but once the routine settled in, he turned into a monster. The New People cannot disobey Angkar. When Angkar tells you to do something, you must do it. Everyone is equal. "Angkar is your Mother and Father," he said. "You must not think about the past anymore. Erase everything you had in the past and don't think about it anymore. There's no rich or poor here. Everyone from now on is equal. We will wear the same kind of clothes. We will eat and work together. When you need to go somewhere, you must ask permission from Angkar."

Black soon became our life's only color—in sleep, while awake, while eating, and even while thinking. From then on, no one was allowed to wear colors, not even shoes or eyeglasses with colors. Angkar would not be content until all traces of imperialism and the bourgeoisie were eliminated. Young girls were ordered to cut their long hair and to work alongside men, as their equals, with no leisure or beauty rest. All of us were the same, with short hair and black clothes, fitted for moving earth and plowing the rice paddies. No one was excused from the drudgery of a peasant's life.

We had each been given a checkered *krama*, a black shirt, and a pair of black pajama-like pants. The checkered *krama* became the symbol of the Khmer Rouge. The black uniform became our way of life. If we wore colored shirts, or pants, we might be taken to be "re-educated," because it would be clear we had not given up the "civilized" way of life. Aside from that one outfit, this all-black wardrobe was our responsibility to create. My parents didn't know how to dye clothes—they were used to going to the market and bargaining for ready-made clothes, fresh from the factory, in a choice of sizes and colors to satisfy their tastes. But an old woman took pity on us and showed us how to dip our fabrics into natural dyes. And so we entered the colorless world of the Khmer Rouge.

At the nightly meetings, after they were finished telling us what they wanted us to know, they'd ask if anyone had questions or suggestions. A few people said yes, and they were taken somewhere. The Khmer Rouge pretended that they liked those people for getting up and giving suggestions or making their dissatisfaction known. We never saw those people again. They wanted everybody who was a part of a revolutionary society to be pure of mind. If we flouted their rules in any way, the Khmer Rouge told us Angkar would punish us. We soon came to understand that the punishment was death.

Then the Khmer Rouge broke up our families. Most of the young adults were sent off to labor camps. All of my brothers except Da, and all of my sisters were told to pack and leave the next day. My mother knew the labor camp would be a torturous place, and people would die from overwork and starvation. She cried and told them to take care of themselves and, whatever happened, to come back to Tuk Chjo village to reunite with their family if given the chance. The soldiers came and took them. I was only seven. Among the children in our family, only Da and I were left. I couldn't understand what was going on. In my house, only the little children and the elderly were left. My parents were assigned to work by digging irrigation canals. I had to work pulling weeds in the fields. People began to suffer from malaria, diarrhea, cholera, and infection. During the rainy season, when people died, there was no dry land for burial, so the bodies were thrown into the river.

When we ran out of food, the Khmer Rouge gave us rations. Once a day, each person got a cup of rice and some salt and nothing else. During the night, Father, Da, and I took our mosquito net and used it to gather shrimp and fish. When it was the planting season, food was scarce so they gave us just one cup of rice per family instead of per person. At night, village spies watched and listened. We had a curfew. By nine o'clock everyone had to be asleep. Those who were heard talking about the past would be taken in the middle of the night never to be seen again.

One boy I knew had been stealing palm juice every night because he didn't get enough to eat. Every day, an older village man climbed up the palm tree with several bamboo canisters to retrieve the juice. He would cut the flower bud of the palm and put the bamboo canisters underneath them to let the juice drip into them overnight. This kid had been keenly observing, and took the sweet juice from the canisters to fill his starved belly. The owner of the juice eventually found out and informed the Khmer Rouge of his loss. One night, a couple of Khmer Rouge soldiers were waiting for the boy to come down from the tree. When he did, the Khmer Rouge didn't question him. They just beat him up, tortured him with their bayonets, broke his bones, and then killed him. He was left there unburied. When his mother found out the next day, she screamed violently and her tears dripped on her son's broken body. His blood was dried and his skin yellowed and swollen. He was her only son, and as she was trying to dig the earth with her fingernails to bury him, the Khmer Rouge came to fetch her. They didn't want anyone mourning the dead. That would be a sign of weakness. So they killed her as well. They said they were doing her a favor by letting her join her dead son.

At the next education meeting, the Khmer Rouge used the boy and his mother as examples of the enemies of Angkar, telling us that anyone who dared to commit such a crime would be punished. "No one steals from Angkar," they warned. We always felt very insecure at these meetings. The Khmer Rouge seemed to stare with suspicion at my parents and at me. Angkar apparently didn't believe that we had been poor, because we looked Chinese and had light skin. To them, we looked like people who had experienced too much leisure. We belonged to the wealthy class. The night they came for my parents, I felt that they would kill them and leave me to die a slow death by starvation. But they only wanted to question them to see if they were telling the truth. My father never said much to us after that incident. He shut himself up, even from us, as if he were deaf and mute.

Another night, Angkar called a meeting of all the children. Parents were told to stay home. This time my parents thought that they would never see *us* again. All their lives they had worked hard to serve us, to care for us, and to secure a good future for us. Mother devoted all her life to rearing us and helping us grow into good human beings. Suddenly they had no control over what would happen to us. Our destiny was in the hands of Angkar. My mother could not complain or show any sign of resistance or protest. Angkar saw all and punished all for any deviance in the new society.

Once again, the Khmer Rouge children were tasked with reminding us who we were. They looked at us, the New People, with sharp eyes. The Khmer Rouge kept their eyes closely on men and women from the city. The fields and all the land and rivers belonged to the Old People, born of earth and water, and they had authority over us. They were free to roam about and their children could run and play. They could mock me by calling me names and saying I was useless. They didn't think I could survive the life they had because I was born into a wealthy existence, one they believed once had authority over them.

"You Chinese!" they would scream and laugh. "You can't cultivate rice. You know nothing but leisure."

The leader instructed us to abandon any feelings of belonging to our parents. "Angkar," he said, "is your parent now."

I didn't think I could ever ignore my parents and say that they were strangers to me. I could never detach myself from my mother, especially. She was the only person I felt safe with. I didn't think I could ever deny my own father, either. But at the children's meeting, all of us were called up to a blackboard and forced to erase ourselves from the family of the past. Pictures of parents holding hands with children were cut at the hands to show this break in ownership. Angkar was our parent now and all children had to show commitment only to Angkar.

SEVEN

Blood of My Blood

Several months later, the village leader and his comrades began a more severe purge of those they felt were enemies of Angkar. Those perceived as suspicious or different in any way were tied to trees or posts and tortured, and then killed. Sometimes we heard screams at night and the sound of whips striking people.

Most of the Khmer Rouge couldn't read or write. They had a lot of hatred toward us because we came from a different lifestyle and had controlled the former government, which they considered corrupt. The Khmer Rouge especially resented the rich, the educated, former government officers, and the Buddhist laypeople. In the old days, Cambodians with wealth and social status often looked down on the poor, while Hinduism and Buddhism explained that being poor was a matter of fate. One was born poor or born rich. But the rich exploited the poor and made them their servants. For centuries, being a peasant meant that you were not educated and were not as worthy as other people. The Khmer Rouge were therefore following the Maoist agrarian plan to eliminate this kind of inequality. They wanted to rid society of those who looked down on others. As they saw it, killing the rich and destroying religion was an act of revenge against classicism and social divisions.

One trick strategy they used against those they suspected were not complying with their ideology was to force people to lie about their past occupation. The Khmer Rouge would torture people for a false confession—or a false accusation against their neighbor, either one—and then kill them. My father tried to keep a low profile so he would not be outed. When the Khmer Rouge tested him to see if he could read or write, he pretended to write like a child.

Every evening after dinner, the Khmer Rouge guards called all the New People to the meeting. A desk was set in the middle of an open field. All the important leaders sat behind this desk, speaking with great authority. Nobody would dare talk back. Nobody was allowed to speak except them. The New People sat on the ground quietly listening to their revolutionary rhetoric. The meeting was usually long and tiring. The leaders would say the same things over and over, addressing one another formally as Comrade This and Comrade That. They seemed to mention Angkar with every breath.

"Angkar fought very hard to destroy the old system," they said. "That old system was very corrupt, materialistic, and divided those who were rich and those who were poor. Now there is only one. Angkar you must trust. Angkar wants everyone to be equal, no rich and no poor. We must be collective in everything we do. We eat, sleep, work together, and wear the same clothes. You must forget about the past. If anyone is dissatisfied with the work of another, you need to bring it up at the meeting. Angkar will help you solve your problem."

Mother and Father told them the story that we had been homeless junk collectors at the mercy of the wealthy class. That did not actually turn out to be a very good lie. Our family's soft hands and light complexion did not match the past we described, and the

Khmer Rouge began to watch us very closely. Everything about us was brought into question. My father worried that his true identity would become his greatest enemy.

And then, late one night, Angkar came for him. We heard footsteps on the bamboo stairway and woke up in fear. Mother knew then that they must be coming for one of us. Two or three men, in the dark, invaded our house, looking for my father. It was pitch-black and one of them lit a cigarette lighter to scan the room, seeing our frightened eyes. They called out my father's name and we knew then that he would be killed. These soldiers were young, none of them older than my brothers San and Reth. "The leader wants to talk to you," they told my father. Why now? my mother thought, but she was afraid to say it out loud. "It's late," Father said. "Could it wait until the morning?" But he obeyed and went with them. "Don't worry," he whispered. "I'll be back soon."

"He will come back soon," the soldiers told us. "Don't follow. If anyone is caught following or dares to scream for help, then all of you will have to meet Angkar, too."

After they took Father, we started to cry as though he were already dead. We waited for him, but he did not return. Mother was still in tears, imagining where they had taken him or what they would do to him. That night, she stayed awake, haunted by the fear of his death. I tried to fall sleep beside her. I couldn't understand what had happened or what would happen to me without my parents.

In the morning, Mother went to work in the fields as usual, hoping her husband would appear there beside her, sowing the rice that looked dirty in their light-skinned hands. I sat on the doorstep hoping to see him return. I used to wait for him after work, and he'd always come back with a happy smile to see me. This time, I waited longer than usual. But he had been taken, and all my waiting was of no use.

A few days later, I thought I saw my father coming home. When I called out to him, he was gone. He disappeared into the setting sun. His smile evaporated as I was about to call out, "Father! Father!" My mother told me that I was just missing my father. "Go get your food," she said.

The food bell rang. I took my mother's teakettle and ran for my portion. I was thinking of how my father, Da, and I would take our mosquito net down to the river to catch small fish and shrimps to add to our meager dinner and then how Da and I warned our parents when we saw the Khmer Rouge coming to inspect our dinner. But after several days went by, it finally sank in , and I knew my father was not coming back. Mother was a widow. She tried not to show her emotions because the Khmer Rouge would kill her if she did. I thought a lot about my mother and what would happen to me if they came to take her, too.

Each day had the same sense of hopeless annihilation. My stomach growled with hunger all the time. Many people had already died. The large crowd of people we'd arrived with had been reduced. Our house was once full. Now, most of the older people had died or been killed. Some had gone to meetings with Angkar and never returned. I didn't understand all this sadness, fear, and darkness. I needed to hear my mother's voice whispering her lullabies to me. Every night, as I slept next to her, she whispered good things to me and Da and told happy stories about our old home in Kampong Speu. She reminded us never to say or do anything against any of Khmer Rouge children. If they tried to hurt us, she said we should be patient and bite our tongues and keep silent. "Soon," she said hopefully, "the country will return to normal."

Three days after he was taken from us, a villager stopped by to confirm our father's death. She told us he had been tortured and murdered. The Kong Chlops, the Khmer Rouge spies, had tied his hands behind his back, forced him into a ditch beyond the pagoda, and killed him. They hit him with a bamboo pole until his neck broke and then shot him to death. The woman said that he had convulsed violently before going completely still. His body was pushed down a small decline near some bamboo bushes.

My mother snuck out late that evening to find his corpse. When she did, she did not scream. She just reached out a hand to touch Father's bruises. His blood had soaked into the dry earth. After her frail evening good-bye, her eyes dark with tears, she buried him in a shallow grave near the bamboo bushes. When she returned home, she avoided talking to us about it.

Several weeks later, my brother Reth returned from the work camp he'd been put in. He was too gaunt and sickly to go back to it, so the leader allowed him to work in the temple. His job was to destroy all the stupas and the Buddha statues and turn them to gravel. He was also forced to make fertilizer out of cow dung and human feces. I remember sleeping between Reth and Mother one night under a bright moon and listening to Reth whisper about his horrible experiences at the work camp. After he fell asleep, he had a sudden vision in which he saw Father standing by the window, smiling. He woke up screaming, pointing hysterically toward the ghost of our father. "Your father came to say good-bye," Mother told him. "He is in a good place now. Go back to sleep. Your father is OK."

Several days later, Reth died. He went calmly in his sleep. Father must have come and taken him, I thought. Maybe it was better that way. He wasn't beaten and tortured to death. He left of his own free will. His spirit had gone to another life, and we hoped it was a better life than this one. Mother kept shaking him. "Son, wake up!" When he didn't wake up, her hand weakened and she collapsed onto his still body. I could see how pale his flesh was. He had been gaunt, helpless, with no blood bringing color to his body. He left us thinking of our own deaths, of how fate would unite us again one day.

The village leader didn't oppose my mother's burying Reth, so we dragged his body to a spot of ground where we could feed it to the earth. Tears had exhausted us emotionally, while lack of food had weakened us physically. I kept thinking of all the good food we used to have before this interruption of our lives. I especially missed chicken curry with French bread, freshly baked from a clay oven, and the other freshly baked breads Mother would get from the market. Reth's body was buried near the swamp behind the temple.

It was just the beginning of yet another level of blackness. The fear of death preoccupied us as we ate less and less food and worked more and more in the field. Mother received news that my sister Mohm had died at the Khmer Rouge's hospital in Tuk Chjo village. Mother rushed to the hospital after returning from the field on that evening, but Mohm's body was gone. It was a rainy day, and the water flowed over the river bank into everywhere in the village. There was no dry area, and the Khmer Rouge had no way to bury Mohm. She was not buried. We could only assume that she had been thrown into the river. There was no news of my other siblings. Mother was choked with sadness. Every evening, I witnessed my mother's eyes swelling in pain and grief over the loss of her children. Reth and Mohm had died, and we hadn't heard about San, Theary and Chan. The fate of my other three siblings who were living in the city before the Khmer Rouge took over was still not known. We had no idea which part of the country they had gone to. We were thinking of them and hoping they would stay alive to be reunited with us someday. Weeks and months had gone by ever so slowly, with drudgeries and despair, and death was like an ordinary event. Every day, someone died. I was afraid of dying. I didn't want to die yet. But I could feel it all around me, dead people and their starvation.

My house, which doesn't belong to me, is full of ghosts, I thought. One by one they go, dying of hunger and torture. Each morning, there is a dead body on the front step, with no one to care. It is just one of those no one wants to bury. It's too heavy to lift. What can we do? We can't even lift ourselves to work. Let the leaders deal with it. Tell them, "Comrade, there is a dead man over there." They will send a few of their men to drag the body away. Life is nothing to them. The dead have no family to mourn over them. No one is allowed to grieve anyway. Death is death. The Khmer Rouge don't care. They don't respect the body and give it dignity or ceremony. They don't believe in religion. To them, religion is superstition. "Throw the body somewhere," they will say. "Take it away and throw it in the bushes to rot. Make sure we don't smell it."

The Khmer Rouge had by now reduced our rice ration to half a cup every day for each family. With this rice Mother would make a porridge mixed with bindweeds. Sometimes, when Da and I went swimming, we would still secretly gather shrimp and fish with our mosquito net, as we had done with Father. If the Khmer Rouge knew we were doing this, they would have taken us to be killed. Whatever we caught, we hid inside our clothes. Still, we grew gaunt and malnourished.

Some of the New People screamed in their sleep because of their hunger. Sometimes the very next morning they died, though fighting to stay alive, their hands dancing in the dark, posturing to Buddha for mercy. Every bit of their flesh had been absorbed by their hunger. Only their bones remained. Our crowded thatched house had been reduced to an open space of a few bodies fighting dark dreams. I thought it was better to die of starvation than to be axed or battered by a log of bamboo. I wanted to go like my brother, in my sleep. That was my hope.

I noticed that the Old People always had enough to eat. We were the refugees, the city people robbed of home and land. In their eyes, we didn't deserve to have enough. They wanted to teach us how it felt to have nothing.

The lack of food got so bad that Da sneaked out in the middle of the night in search of sweet potatoes, raw bamboo, and sugarcane to give energy to his body so that he could work the next morning. He wanted to save himself and our family, but he wasn't a good thief. A young Khmer Rouge his own age caught him and took him away, with his hands tied behind his back, just as they done my father. When I saw this, I followed them to see where he was being taken. I stood at a distance looking on, praying that they would spare his life. I wanted to run after them and free him as they were questioning and beating him.

"Here is another thief," the boy said to the leader. "He tries to steal bamboo shoots from Angkar." One of the Khmer Rouge kept hitting Da with his rifle while he was forced to kneel and beg the leader, who sat on his doorstep with his legs crossed, like a king, for forgiveness.

"Please, I was hungry. I am sorry. I didn't mean to steal from Angkar." Da clasped his hands together as he prostrated himself in front of the leader. The leader sat there laughing as he smoked a cigarette.

"Didn't we tell you not to steal from the beginning? Everything belongs to Angkar. Not to you alone." He kicked my brother in the face as if he were a dog.

"Now, you take the bamboo shoots and plant them back into the ground. If the bamboo does not grow back, you will die."

One of the soldiers took his rifle and started to beat Da on his back. Da was in pain and struggled to get up. I heard him groan. Then he called, "Oh, Mother, please help!" His face was full of tears, crying, and I could see he was in pain. I wished I could do something, but I knew I would be killed if I tried to save him. I stood there and felt the pain they were inflicting on Da and wiped my tears. I'd thought the Khmer Rouge might shoot him right there, and I was so relieved when they let him go. "Now, go," the leader said. "Next time, don't take things that don't belong to you."

Nobody had planted that bamboo that Da took. Bamboo grows naturally, and people dig out the shoots when they emerge from the ground, especially when it rains. You can make good soup out of bamboo shoots. My mother used to prepare a curry of shoots with pork and would take it as an offering to the monks. It was one of my favorites.

My brother replanted the bamboo shoots in the place where

he'd gotten them. They never grew back. Bamboo, once cut, doesn't grow back. Fortunately, weeks later, the leaders had forgotten all about it. My brother was lucky. His life was spared. After that, Da was afraid to steal food.

One evening, a Me-Kong, a camp leader who was in charge a large group of people, and a Me-Krum, a supervisor of a group of ten to twenty workers, went around to all the houses and ordered people to turn over all the valuables they had, including their own pots and pans, for the good of the community. The Khmer Rouge searched every house and dispossessed people of their belongings. Nothing belonged to us—just the black clothes on our bodies, which were to be considered gifts from Angkar. When my mother heard this, she took our family pictures and all the jewelry she had saved and buried them. My mother's Me-Krum came into our home yelling, "Give them up! Where are your pots and pans? Whatever you brought with you from the city, you must give to Angkar."

In my mother's kitchen, there were a few pots and pans she had dragged with her through our long journey. They were the few things that made her feel closest to home. She had fed her family meals she had lovingly prepared with them. The Me-Krum piled the pots and pans on the ground, and even took our spoons, forks, and knives. Without them, we had nothing to cut with, no ability to cook whatever we foraged to eat or boil our drinking water to avoid dysentery. Da was lying sick as this Khmer Rouge woman invaded our home, looking with her snake eyes for whatever possessions we might have.

"Angkar would not let you die, so don't worry," she affirmed. I wanted to stab her with the knife she'd picked up from our kitchen floor. The community would never give us enough to eat. How could she tell us not to worry?

My mother begged to keep just the teakettle. "Please, comrade, may I keep this teapot to boil water for my son? Look, he is very sick. I beg of you. I want him to get better so that he can work for Angkar." Da could not talk, so my mother pointed to my brother's swollen body.

"All right, you can keep that teakettle and nothing else," the Me-Krum said. "You may also have one spoon each and a bowl for the food Angkar will give you. Let me remind you that tomorrow morning, there will be a meeting before you head out to the field. From now on, everyone must eat together and you should get your food from the group that you're assigned to."

She was not done. In our sleep area, the Me-Krum searched our bags by emptying everything onto the floor. There was nothing of value for her to take. After my father and Reth died, my mother stuffed their clothes in those bags. All things of value to my mother were hidden away underground, behind some bushes near the house.

The whole village was seized by the sounds of those searches as the Khmer Rouge collected all our goods and stripped us of any sense of a private life. The clanging of pots and pans was like a death knell for any ownership. All the children belonged to Angkar. Everyone must work for Angkar. When it was time to eat, we must run like a group of baby chicks to the feeding line. We anxiously waited with our bowls, which we clutched for a ladle full of rice porridge.

At that time, I was eight years old, and Da about ten. The Khmer Rouge made us work in the fields so hard and long with only that bowl of watery rice to eat twice a day. From morning to darkness we worked, ate what was given to us, and sat at meetings to recondition our brains to think in Angkar's ways. They told us, "From now on you are forbidden to light a fire in your own house." We were supposed to feel our way in the dark to find the stairs. There were no candles or lanterns. We lived days and nights in our black clothes. If anyone was found cooking, it was everyone's duty to report that person to the Me-Krum. Angkar would take them away for reeducation. It was a crime, and once you had been taken, you never returned.

Da kept swelling up as they continued to deprive him of proper nourishment. He and I worked in the same area, but in different groups, so I would see him but could never talk to him. Our leader kept strict watch as we dug the dirt to make irrigation canals. A line of us, children with tender hands and frail bodies, dug the earth and passed it along in bamboo baskets to build an embankment to block off the flow of water and irrigate the rice fields.

Near the temple Wat Tuk Chjo, Buddha statues were desecrated and laughed at by the Khmer Rouge children. Then they were thrown into the pond, as a symbolic way of destroying all beliefs. Angkar did not believe in any religion except the revolution. Back home in Kampong Speu, my mother had taught me to respect my religion, parents, and older siblings. The Khmer Rouge children had no respect for anything at all. Their parents never taught them to respect or care about other people. In my heart, I kept on praying, hoping Buddha would bring us back those better days, free to worship all things we loved and valued. I would think of how devout my mother was to the Buddha, whom Angkar was trying to erase from all memory. The Buddha was the strength of my mother's soul and no matter what they told me, I still believed, just as my mother did, in the Buddha of compassion. From a distance, I extended my sympathy and my love to Da, who was working in slow motion as he grew weaker and weaker.

The Me-Kong and Me-Krum sat in their hammocks while we worked, watching us with their rifles ready. A boy was seen catching a mouse and was ordered by the Me-Kong to get out of the field. When the boy stopped what he was doing, the Me-Kong came up to him and smacked him with his AK-47. The boy fell to the ground unconscious as others kept working in their silence, pretending not to see or hear the crack of the gun or that boy's pain. He was about my age. I resolved that I would never be caught stealing.

EIGHT

Mother's Last Words

With the coming of the dry season, my mother became very ill. All around us, the New People were dying from overwork and malnutrition. They had never worked so hard in all their lives. They had never before gone a day without a good meal. When I was a boy in Ang Sarey, I was always sure that my mother would prepare something for me as soon as I woke up. Now she was dying. Father had been killed. Reth and Mohm had died. Da was getting sicker and sicker. His belly ballooned like a blowfish, so badly swollen I thought I could take a pin and poke the air out of him. His skin was all blistered, his hands were skin and bones, eyelids swollen, face disfigured. I hoped the new leaders would give him some sympathy, but the Khmer Rouge didn't care if you were gaunt and weak. We still had to work. We had to overcome our miseries and go out into the fields, plowing away in the hot sun with nothing in our stomachs to keep us going.

It was a slow death. People were walking skeletons, their eyes so deeply sunken into their sockets that I couldn't tell who was who. Every day I saw dead bodies wrapped in blankets taken away to be thrown into the river, fed to the fish, or left behind bushes of bamboo to rot. The Buddhist temple of Tuk Chjo had become a dumping ground. But the dead who were thrown there were luckier than the ones thrown in the river—at least they were on holy ground. Maybe it wasn't holy to the Khmer Rouge, but it was to us, to me. I felt that my father was in a good place, although I wouldn't dare go near his grave—the Khmer Rouge would claim I was still attached to him. They said I belonged to Angkar. I was Angkar's child. I had no father or mother.

As the second year wore on, all New People received just one small bowl of watery rice porridge a day and a little salt once a week. They gave us the salt only because they needed us to work the fields. A bowl of tasteless rice porridge was never enough for my needs as a growing boy; I managed to stay alive by stealing.

Whenever we went to the community food line, nobody talked to anyone else. We would sit in silence, sipping the ladle full of rice porridge we'd been given. So many of us had died of malaria, diarrhea, and swelling. Our skin yellowed. Our sense of taste had disappeared. After my rice porridge, I never felt as though I had eaten anything. The porridge was very thin, with only a few cups of rice spread among a few thousand people, although that number was eventually reduced by starvation to just hundreds. The weaker we were, the harder the Khmer Rouge forced us to work. The fruit of our labor was for Angkar, not for us.

In addition to death from starvation, there were periodic executions. Almost every day, I heard screams from people being tortured and gunshots from people being executed—those who received the bullets were luckier than those who were tortured. How could I have been born into this? I wondered. Why am I being punished with this misfortune?

My dear mother was getting weaker and weaker, her frail body fading. Still, she was told to work. There was plenty of rice for everyone, but it was sent to Angkar. My mother harvested it with her hands. There were fields upon fields of rice. The land was fertile and kind, but the Khmer Rouge weren't. They took from us our rights to have what we labored for. With their guns, they could demand whatever they wanted. Day and night, the Khmer Rouge had us cut rice with our machetes and thresh it in the field. In the evening, they would load the rice onto trucks. We never knew where all the rice we sowed and harvested went.

Late one afternoon, Mother came home so exhausted that she couldn't even climb the steps to the house. I heard her call for help.

"Help me, son, I've fallen."

"Da!" I called out to my brother. "Help! Mother is very weak. Please, hurry." I wasn't strong enough to help her by myself. I felt so bad seeing her like that, on the ground, unable to move, her skeletal frame, her face aged ten years beyond its time.

Da was himself very weak. His face was yellowed from lack of salt, and his whole body was swollen from malnutrition. He walked very slowly because of the swelling. The two of us tried to pull our mother up the steps and carry her into the house. We didn't know what to do. All we did was cry. I shook her slightly, hoping she would open her eyes. She was unconscious.

"Mother, please don't die," I begged. Da's swollen eyes had enough tears to flood the world with his pain. If Mother goes, I thought, Da will be the only person I have left. But if things don't get better, he, too, may go, and I'll be left stranded on this mad earth, with only my heart in a violent convulsion.

Mother did not move. There was no sign of her breathing.

"Oh, Buddha, please don't let her go," I prayed. We went to one of the neighbors, an old woman, for help.

"Our mother is very sick," we told her. "Please, help us." The old woman took pity on us. She belonged to one of the Khmer Rouge families. After we cried and begged for her support, she came to our house to check on our mother. She felt Mother's pulse and told us she would be OK.

"Coin her," she told us. "She'll be fine." I took a coin of old money from Mother's secret bundle to do what the old woman had suggested. People throughout Cambodia scrape their bodies with coins when they get sick to help with their healing, especially when there is no medicine, so I poured water on my mother's bony body and started to scrape. Usually we would use Tiger Balm instead of water, because it is a lubricant and less painful, but we didn't have any. My mother probably couldn't feel the pain anyway. She lay there without moving, almost dead. I wished we had some real medicine. My father had brought a lot of modern medicines with us from Kampong Speu, but we'd used them up during the forced marches. And Western medicine was considered an enemy to the Khmer Rouge, anyway. The old woman suggested that I go and find some herbs. I said I didn't know where to look for herbs. She told me she had some in her backyard. I gathered some roots and some twigs of a particular tree to boil for my mother to drink. Without the old woman's help, I would not have known what to do.

What Mother really needed, though, was enough to eat and some time to rest. While Da was coining her, I started the fire to boil the roots. I realized that it was time to receive our food ration. The bell had struck three times.

"Get our rations, too, for me and mother," Da said. I grabbed our three bowls. When I got there, I was the first in line. But the young Khmer Rouge woman in charge of the rations told me that every person must come for the food him or herself.

"No show, no food," she said.

She could not have been more than fifteen years old. Everything about her was dark. Her skin and cow-like eyes were fed with dark blood.

"But my brother and mother are at home sick," I pleaded. "Please, give them some food." She gave me only my portion, a small scoop of rice, along with a dirty, hateful look. I kept standing there, begging her to give me two other scoops for my mother and brother. As I held the bowls up to her face, she reached down with a ladle and knocked me on the head. I felt a sharp pain, a chilled hurt inside, but I tried not to cry. She took no pity on my soft, small eyes and my frail, begging hands. My mother would not get any food because she was lying sick in the house. My brother couldn't walk because he was too swollen up.

"What do you keep standing here for?" she yelled. Her well-fed hand shooed me away as if I were a sick dog. "Go! Didn't I tell you that your mother and brother must come to get the ration themselves?"

I ran all the way home, panting and holding back the tears with the thought that I would have to divide my scoop of rice between the three of us. Mother began to open her eyes a little bit. At least she was still alive.

"Is Mother OK, Da," I asked?

"She cannot speak," he said. "She is so weak. I think she wants to tell us something. Did you get our food?"

"No, Da. You must run quickly and get it yourself, at least your portion of it. That woman won't give it to me. She said that we each have to go and get it ourselves. Go! Run quickly before it's too late."

Da dragged himself slowly to get the food. If he wasn't able to get his share, I was willing to give up my portion for Mother and him. But Da did get his portion, and I gave my entire portion to Mother. My brother offered me some of his, but I told him to have all of it. It wasn't even enough for him. His swelling was getting worse each day.

I couldn't go to sleep hungry. I had to find something. It was around eight and it was dark out. I decided that I must go and forage for something to eat. My stomach was growling and my thoughts were only of food, like fresh, bourgeois French bread, rice, and pudding.

I told Da that I was going out to take a crap. In truth, I didn't know where I was going. I was so afraid of being caught. I had witnessed what they did to that boy for stealing juice and my brother for stealing bamboo shoots. Dire hunger forced me to take my chances. I was too hungry. The night was moonlit, so at least I could see where I was going. I had to walk lightly so that I wouldn't make any sound. I could see the crescent moon above, and I prayed to it to help me find something to fill me up for the night. Behind my house, across this muddy swamp, were private pastures and gardens that belonged to the Old People. As I was searching for these small gardens, mosquitoes bit deeply into me. The swamp was a breeding ground for them. I also smelled the rotten bodies of the people who'd been killed. It didn't bother me. All I could think of was food, and the fear that I might be caught by one of the Khmer Rouge spies, the Kong Chlops. These people were the all-seeing eyes of Angkar, the police of the village. If one of them caught me, he would beat me, just as they had beaten my brother for stealing the bamboo shoots. Or worse. I was very surprised they let Da go. Usually, when they caught people stealing food, they would beat them to death.

I came to a farm of sweet potatoes and dug my fingers in the dirt in search of the sweet roots. The soil for growing sweet potatoes has to be soft, so it was easy for me to get the potatoes without pulling out the whole plant. I lay flat on my stomach and kept myself hidden in the bushes. In the dim moonlight, I shoved my hands into the earth to gather the potatoes that I felt were rightfully mine. I hadn't grown them, but I deserved to have them inside of me for my sustenance. I didn't wait to clean them with water. I ate some raw, while I put others in my *krama*. I gathered another handful of sweet potatoes for Da and my mother. I also picked some oranges, and wrapped everything my checkered *krama*. I sat in the dark bushes for a few minutes to see if any Kong Chlops were watching for me. I told myself I must not make any noise. I lowered my head and walked on my tiptoes as silently as I could. My eyes moved around like a robot's, scanning for any movement. Whenever I stepped on sharp sticks or thorns, I held my breath and bit my tongue. I was so afraid of being caught. As soon I arrived near my house, I saw some Kong Chlops patrolling along the road, smoking cigarettes. I waited a few minutes until they passed, then ran into the house. Da was shocked, seeing me return with such fear on my face. He thought I had just gone to the bathroom behind the house, but instead I'd returned with a bundle of sweet potatoes and oranges.

"Da! Da!" I whispered, "I've got these oranges and potatoes from the garden." I didn't want Da to ask me out loud what garden I had been to because I was afraid Kong Chlops might be spying on us from below our house. We were burning the fire so we could take care of our sick mother and the Kong Chlops could have doubled back to check on us. They made no exception for sickness.

"We'd better hide them quickly," he said. "Hide them under our clothes." My feet were bleeding from stepping on thorns, and thistles had cut many parts of my body. I wasn't conscious of the blood. Nothing hurts more than hunger. Hunger forces you to do just about anything, even risk your own life to steal food. This time, I was lucky and safe.

We made no sound peeling the oranges, washing my bloody feet, or washing the potatoes. It was all done with a cloth. We squeezed drops of the sweet orange into our mother's mouth.

"How did you get these oranges?" she whispered, some of her strength coming back. I didn't answer, though, because I didn't want to make her worry.

"Just eat, Mother. It's OK." I probably didn't have to tell her that I'd stolen them. She knew. My stomach had stopped growling and we all went to sleep peacefully.

It was before dawn when the bell rang for us to go to work. Mother was still very sick. I went to her Me-Krum to ask if she could stay home. The Me-Krum came to check on her. She was lying on the mat, helpless, with no energy, but the Me-Krum told her to go to work anyway.

"I didn't find anything wrong with her," the Me-Krum said. "There's no evidence of swelling or anything. She's fine." Turning to my mother, she said, "You're just lazy, pretending to be sick. Get up and go to work!"

So Mother had to go into the fields. I couldn't understand why the Me-Krum was such a cruel woman. She treated Mother as though she had no worth. It was as if she wanted to work her to her death. What would I do when they took her away from me just as they had taken my father and brother? That question had run through my mind over and over again.

"Hurry, hurry up, Seng, we are late to the field again," Da called. But I didn't want to leave Mother. What would happen if she fell again? I watched her getting up from the floor to try to get ready. I felt so sad and helpless. If I could have been two people and substituted for her, Angkar would have been satisfied.

"Mother is all right," Mother spoke, confidently. Then she hurried me and Da to the field. I wrapped my *krama* around my neck and ran to work. Da couldn't keep up with me. He yelled from behind and told me to slow down for him. I looked back and saw his swollen body lumbering along like an elephant. We didn't know what our Me-Krum would do to us if we were late again. He might give us more work, torture us, or take us to be reeducated.

So many people had already died. I kept thinking of how our house had once been full of people. We had been almost sleeping on top of one another. Now there were only the three of us. The other elders had all died. I had smelled their decaying bodies out in the swamp when I went looking for sweet potatoes. My mother was so gaunt I couldn't recognize her.

There came a point where my mother couldn't stand anymore. The Khmer Rouge hadn't given us anything to eat for three days. It was deep in the monsoon season and the village leader ran out of rice for us to eat. We had to wait a few days for Angkar to supply rice. I thought that the village leaders would keep the rice for themselves and let us starve. Da was all swollen with water, and his belly felt like a rubber balloon that could explode at any time. Death was the only way out of all this suffering. Mother knew it. She was just sorry that she would have to leave us alone, having to find our way in this world. If we were lucky, we would survive to see brighter days. But at that time, everything was dark even when it was a beautiful day and the sky was clear. Time had stopped. There were only memories to fill Mother's heart with grief, and I could take nothing more from my childhood than the sadness in her eyes.

I would never be a child again. I would need to survive like an adult so as not to forget the suffering my mother went through. Her "good-bye" was unbearable in every way and the words she spoke will stay with me until I die. Will I survive to tell our story? I wondered. My mother's hands were cold. Her body had no warmth. I could feel her bones reaching out to me through her skin.

She spoke with great effort. It seemed clear to me that she was preparing to die. "I wish I could stay strong and healthy to see you grow up, my sons," she told us. "But this place has made me too weak. I don't think I can take it anymore. You look out for each other, OK? When I'm gone, Da, you take care of your little brother."

Da was broken himself. "Must you go, Mother?"

"Don't cry, my children. All will pass. You hold on and stay alive. If you ever make it out of here alive, look for your brother in France. He doesn't know what is happening to us."

Her voice got weaker and weaker. It dropped to a melancholy, dying whisper, fading sobs of despair.

"Remember," she said, beginning to reminisce, "when Mother was strong, before the war, I used to make you the best of food. Your favorite, Seng, was French bread dipped in chicken curry. You loved to go shopping with me at the bazaar." She grinned, trying to let out a bit of laughter, but it was just a faint echo. If I could, I would have made her the kind of meal she used to make for us. "Mother used to prepare special food for the holidays," she continued. "Don't you remember? Every morning before you went to school, I used to go out in front of the house to buy fresh French bread for the family. Now Mother doesn't have any food for you to eat. I know that you're hungry, my sons. Mother will go. I won't be able to see you and take care of you anymore. Do you understand?

After I'm gone, Da, you watch after your little brother. Now, Seng, fetch my bag. There's a picture of your brother, Yean, who now lives in France. Should the situation in our country get better, you go and find him in France, you hear?"

During that week when she was the sickest, I went around stealing food to keep her and Da alive. I didn't care anymore if I was caught. Da, by this point, couldn't move either. His swelling had made him handicapped. He wanted to go out looking for food with me, but I told him he wasn't quick enough to run.

"I don't want you to get caught by the Kong Chlops," I told him.

I survived on the food I stole. I didn't care whether I was caught or not. I wanted to do all I could to keep my mother and brother alive.

Three days before her death, the Khmer Rouge wouldn't allow us to stay home to take care of her. Mother was very incredibly sick, but the Khmer Rouge wouldn't allow us to stay home to take care of her, and I didn't want to leave her all by herself. So one morning, Da went off to the field with his group even though his body still swollen. I held back. One of the Me-Krums came to my house and stood right out front calling out to me, "Met Seng, it's time to go to the field. You are late! Everyone has already left. Let's go! Let's go!"

I came out and asked the Me-Krum, who was about fifteen years old, if he would permit me to stay and care for my mother.

"No, there is no need for you to stay," he said. "She is not your mother. Angkar is. Now you belong to Angkar. She is useless to Angkar now. You don't need to take care of her." He gave no sign of human emotion or compassion. He had been reengineered by Maoist ideology. Angkar was the Supreme Ruler over his human soul.

No one could brainwash me into turning against my own mother, not even this son of Angkar. Nothing could undo the love I had for her. He could not tell me that I didn't belong to her. She had given birth to me, nurtured me, and made me the food I loved. How could he say I was not hers? Still, I had no choice but to obey. If I refused to go, I might be killed. They would force me to work myself to death, just like they'd worked my mother. I was so angry at him, but I couldn't show it. I grabbed my *krama*, wrapped it around my neck, and walked off to the field with him.

My group was waiting for us. While I was working, I was thinking of my mother, lying there all by herself with no food to eat, wondering whether or not she could hold on to life long enough to see me when I returned home. While I was handpicking rice, I kept my eyes on my Me-Krum and when he wasn't looking, I stashed some rice where I could return to get it at night.

I came home from the field late that night. It was dark and we had no watch to tell the time. However, I knew exactly when to prepare. My brother and I went to get our regular meal, our scoop of rice porridge. I knew that Mother had saved some gold and a silk sarong for me and I took these things to one of the Old People and traded them for a chicken. The woman took my black *krama* and wrapped the chicken with it so that it didn't make any noise. She looked right and left to make sure the leaders weren't around. If she were caught doing this, the other Khmer Rouge would say she'd betrayed Angkar. "Now, go," she said. "Take the chicken."

I carried this live chicken close to my body to keep it calm so I wouldn't get caught by the Kong Chlops, but it moved so much I decided to kill it by twisting its neck. The poor chicken had its neck broken for our supper, for our medicine. When I got home, I cut it up quickly and put it into the teakettle of boiling water. I covered it with weeds and put the lid on. If the Kong Chlops came to check, I would tell them I was boiling herbal medicine for Mother. It was a quiet night and, thankfully, no one came to see what we were doing. The chicken was a gift from heaven, my mother's special dinner.

"Da, wake Mother up," I said. "The chicken is ready."

"She's too weak," he responded.

"Well, we have to feed her then."

Da and I fed her slowly. She hadn't had food for a while, so we couldn't give her too much at once or she'd be sick. Da held her head up so that I could put a piece of chicken in her mouth.

"Open your mouth, Mother. It's chicken. I got it just for you," I said. She took the first bite of the chicken and smiled.

"It's so delicious, my sons. How did you get the chicken?" she asked.

"I traded it for the gold and the silk sarong that you saved, Mother. This is for you. Please, eat as much you can."

We had almost forgotten what a chicken tasted like. When we finished, we realized we had to somehow get rid of the bones and feathers. It was a full moon and very cool outside. Our stomachs were full for the first time since we had arrived at Tuk Chjo. We didn't know what month or year it was. Stars filled the clear night sky. Da and I sat next to Mother near the window, looking up to heaven, praying for her survival. I was in better shape than my brother was. Alone in my thoughts, I could feel their pain as my own. I wanted to scream, but no one would hear or care about it anyway. I wondered how my sisters and brothers were doing. Were they alive or dead?

"Come closer to me, sons," my mother whispered faintly. "I want to tell you both something."

I knew she was going to try to say good-bye. This was unbearable in every way, and the words she spoke will stay with me until I die.

"What, Mother? You should sleep so you can get your strength back," I said.

"Mother has a few words for you to carry on and remember. Mother might not be able to live until tomorrow."

"Mother, please. You're not going to leave us, are you?" Da and I started to cry.

"Be strong, my sons. Don't you give up hope. Without Mother, you need to move on with your own lives. You are big boys now. I will continue to look after you both."

"How can you look after us when you're gone?" I asked.

"I may not be physically present, but my spirit will be. Don't worry, my sons. Mother will be around to guide you always," she assured us. "Should your older siblings survive, tell them to look after each other. Remember to always try to be a good person, no matter how hateful this world is. Whoever helps you, give them your respect and never forget them. We've lost everything we had, so Mother doesn't have anything to leave or give you except these last words. Don't forget them."

Mother took our hands while tears flowed down her cheeks. The moon was our witness, the stars our friends, waiting to welcome our mother into their spirit world. "Soon," she said, "you will be orphans."

"You can't leave us, Mother," I said. "Da is very sick. I'll be all alone."

"You have to be strong boys and look out for each other. Don't go against Angkar. Pretend not to see though you have eyes. Be mute though you can speak. Be deaf, even though you have ears to hear and a mind to feel. When our country is back to normal, you must go to school to get an education. Education is very important no matter where you go. No one can steal that from you. Always remember our family and avenge for me the pain and suffering they have caused."

After Mother had said these words, she told us to go to sleep. "Don't cry," she said, "or think anything about me. There's no need. I will be fine. It is you I worry about. But you must continue to stay alive. Whatever you do, try to stay alive."

My head felt numb inside from crying. Mother felt my teardrops on her hand because I was sitting right beside her, listening and looking into her eyes. She reached out with her frail hand to wipe away the tears from my skinny cheek. That only made me cry even more.

I wanted to remember everything, her suffering and her pain, the agonies of living like an animal, the enslavement and human cruelty. I told myself to write things down in my mind so that I could live to tell about it one day. I also found some of San's writing in Mother's secret bundle, a small diary that he'd kept in pencil and pen. In it, San described the day we left our home in Kampong Speu and began the long forced journey. I remembered how he used to love writing short stories and drawing cartoons. I thought, if only San were here to describe Mother's heartaches and record what she said to pass on to the family and maybe to the world, so that everyone will remember this cruelty and inhumanity.

Mother was very calm and encouraging. Was Father calling her to go with him? Where was my brother? Maybe they were all around us, but we didn't know it.

"Get some sleep. You have to work in the morning," she said.

I heard the haunting, sorrowful cry of a raven, the bird sent by a demon to take Mother away. He flew above our house and landed on our roof. Wherever this raven went, it seemed, he brought death. He was a messenger. Da and I tried to chase the bird away, but he just sat there, squawking.

"Go away, you evil bird!" we shouted. "Leave our mother alone," But the bird was coming to take Mother to a good place, away from her suffering. We didn't understand—all we knew was that the bird meant death. Before Reth had died, we'd heard the same bird crying above our house. Every time we heard it, a soul was taken. We didn't want it to take our mother. It was so late. Da and I tried to force ourselves to stay awake but finally, exhausted, we fell asleep curled up close to our mother.

Before sunrise, we were awakened by the bell. I cursed the Khmer Rouge! It will all end soon, I thought, and they will all go to hell. I hoped I would live to experience the day when I had enough to eat, a decent place to live, and a chance to go to school. As I tried to open my eyes, sealed shut with dried tears, I saw Mother's blanket covering Da and me. I couldn't be late to the field again, so I went to wash up as quickly as I could. Then I checked on Mother— I always said good-bye to her before I went to work.

"Mother, I'm going to work now. Mother? Mother, wake up!"

I shook her softly.

She didn't move or respond to me. I reached out and felt her cold hand.

"Oh, dear Buddha, my mother. Da, why isn't Mother moving? Wake up. Please, somebody, help my mother. Don't let her die."

Da was frightened.

"She's gone, Da. Mother is dead."

Da's swollen face was getting worse every day and today he looked as though wasps had stung him. We stood there looking at each other with tears in our eyes.

"What do we do?" I asked. "Mother is gone."

"Maybe the old Khmer Rouge woman could help us," Da suggested. I opened the door and ran quickly to get the old woman next door.

"Yay, Yay (grandmother), please help us," I called. "My mother has passed away."

"I'll be right there," she said.

My Me-Krum was standing in front of my house, waiting to remind me that I had duties toward Angkar.

"Met Seng and Met Da, it's time to go to the fields," he said. "You are always late. It's about time for Angkar to reeducate both of you." I hated him and wished I could make him disappear.

"Met, please, could I just stay home for the day? My mother died last night."

"Haven't we told you again and again that she is not your mother anymore? Angkar is. Do you hear me? You have no mother."

"Have pity on the poor boy, son," said the old woman. "Just go and leave him for the day with his mother. She's dead."

My Me-Krum didn't know what to say. He deferred to the old woman and left. I took the old woman by the hand and led her to my mother. Mother's eyes were open, and for a moment I thought she was alive. I trembled at the thought that she might have come back to life. Da was right where I'd left him. His stomach was so swollen that he couldn't walk. He stayed by Mother's side, crying.

"She's gone. Your mother is not coming back," said the old woman.

"Why are her eyes still open?" I asked.

"Sometimes, when people die, their eyes are kept open because they are still missing their loved ones on earth. Her soul is still in the house. She doesn't want to leave you and your brother. She is still thinking of you. She misses you and wants to help you. But she is gone, boys. Your mother is in a good place now. She is resting in peace." She reached down to shut my mother's eyes with her palm.

I didn't want to believe her, but when Mother's eyes were closed and I saw that her face was pale and her body had no sign of life, I finally accepted her passing. Da knew it before I did because he had sat there, watching for any little movement, while I had gone to get the old woman. Mother had no pulse. There was nothing but stillness. The raven had taken her in the night while we were asleep. Mother must have looked at us for the last time and said good-bye. Then she had put her blanket over us so that we could be warm.

"What do we do, Grandmother? Where do we take her?" The old woman had done a lot for us. We always went to her, and she always knew what to do.

"Say a few words to her and cover her with the blanket," she told us. "Go to your Me-Krum and Me-Kong and tell them that your mother has died. Try and get some help to bury her." Then she left.

Da and I dipped our *kramas* into the water from our teapot and began to wash Mother. Out of her bundle I took the traditional clothes she used to wear to the Buddhist temple and dressed her. She had not worn these clothes since that New Year's on April 15, 1975. I wiped her face and eyelids. She looked so skinny. Her eye sockets were so deep and her arms so thin. Her ribs showed through her skin. I unpacked Mother's suitcase to get her dressed up for burial. Then Da took the blanket and put it over her.

"Go and find a new life, Mother, a life as far away from here as possible," I said. Da could not speak. He just kept crying. I remembered going to the temple with my mother and observing how people sat to pray, and so I told Da to clasp his hands, sit cross-legged, and think of good thoughts to send to accompany Mother on her journey. We didn't have any incense. The Khmer Rouge had incense, but not for religious purposes—only to keep mosquitoes away.

One day, Mother, I thought, I will give you a proper ceremony and good-bye. Monks will send you songs from their holy books. Those who know you will gather with flowers at your grave. There will be food and wine for you to share with all the spirits and I will burn a thousand candles in honor of your grace.

"We need to tell the village leader," Da said.

"Yes. I will go over to his house," I said. "I will go and find help to bury Mother, too. You wait here."

I went to the house of village leader, who was smoking his tobacco rolled up inside of a leaf. I told him that my mother had died and I needed his permission to bury her.

He responded almost with a grin and said, "Go and get somebody to help you. Maybe one of your neighbors could help."

Most of the New People were gone, though. Those who remained were the Khmer Rouge. I went to one of the Kong Chlops, but he told me to ask somebody else. I went to a neighbor's house.

"Met Bong," I said, "Big Brother, please help me. My mother died last night. Could you please help me carry her body so we can bury her? My brother cannot walk. I am too small to carry her by myself. Please, help. I will give you a shirt, anything I have for your service." The man acted as if he hadn't heard me. He turned his back and pretended to fix his farm tools while I stood there begging persistently. Finally, the old woman heard my plea. She came out of her house and told the man to help. He agreed and told me to go home and wait for him.

Da and I waited into the afternoon and he didn't show up. We sat there staring at our dead mother, covered with a flannel blanket. The sun burned through the thatched roof. There had been no funeral. There were no friends or relatives to help console us in our grief. And we hadn't eaten yet.

Why would I want to continue living in this place? I thought. Mother, I want to go with you. You should have taken us both with you!

Da was still in tears. All my tears were dried up; I had cried them all while Mother told us her good-bye. Finally the man and his wife came to pick up Mother's body. First, they rolled up her body inside the blanket and tied ropes around it. Then they rolled the body inside a bamboo mat and carried it away on their shoulders. We followed them to the burial ground. Da walked very slowly behind me. It was so hot that I could see the heat waves moving. The earth was dry. The workers were digging and plowing in the fields. Back home in Ang Sarey, I'd noticed that monks and nuns, friends and relatives would always accompany the dead. There was none of that for Mother. I consoled myself with the thought that at least she hadn't been tortured or maimed. Da was out of breath quickly. We stopped, and the man and his wife walked ahead in search of a spot to bury the body. I ran after them. "Please, take her body and bury her next to my father, somewhere by the temple, the right side of it, behind some bamboo bushes. Over there." I pointed.

The man and his wife did not say anything to me, but they moved in that direction, dug a small, shallow hole, dumped my mother's body in it like a log, as if she didn't deserve any honor, and left. The hole was too small. Half of her body was left sticking out, exposed to the heat. They left us with the shovels to continue on our own if we wanted to. Da and I dug as much as we could and then pushed and pulled our mother's body into the hole as though she was a thing just like a cat or a dog, an object. There was nothing reverent or respectful about it; it was meaningless. Finally, her whole body fit into this shallow grave. We gathered small rocks, leaves, and fragments of bamboo branches to cover her and to protect her body from animals.

Da and I placed incense sticks on the head of the grave. We clasped our hands, and kneeled in prayer, remembering our mother's words. "You will be orphans when I am gone," she'd said, "but I will always be with you. My spirit will watch over you. You take good care of each other."

"Good-bye, Mother," I prayed. *"May you rest in peace. I hope you will never come back to this kind of misery ever again. Please, keep watch over us. Help Da regain his strength and make his swelling go away. He's all I have now."*

Da poured his last handful of dirt on our mother and in the hole where our father had been dumped. "Let's go home," he said.

That evening, Da and I sat on the steps of the house until the sun set. We didn't want to go inside. The house would be very empty. We ate our ration of rice soup. We looked at each other but did not say a word.

That night, Mother visited me in a dream. She came down like an angel from heaven, in her beautiful embroidered clothes, to remind me to be strong. I went back to Kampong Speu to our old home, watching myself play and laugh with other children, and she was there, smiling.

"Remember," she said. "Mother will protect you wherever you are and help you in everything you do. You must not give up, but fight for your life."

"Mother! Mother, please don't go!" I screamed in the middle of the night. Da shook me awake.

"Little Brother, Little Brother, wake up. You're just having a nightmare."

"I saw Mother, Da. She was with me."

"Go back to sleep. Everything will be OK. She's with us always," he said.

I couldn't sleep. I kept thinking of her and how in the morning I would have to go back out into the field to work. I took out San's diary and wrote down my dream. The moon was my light, and my mother was one of the stars.

NINE

Bitter Tea

It was the beginning of the rainy season and the monsoon fogged up the countryside. Da's body had become even more swollen. He was dying.

"Seng, do you want to go with me?" he asked quietly one night.

"Where?" I said.

"Go with me to the hospital," he said. "Why do you need to go there?" I asked.

"To get food. The Me-Krum says sick people can get food there. "I'm not allowed to get my portion with my group," he said. Let's go before it's gone. I am very hungry. I need your help to walk there." Da's swollen legs could barely carry him.

I hadn't known they were feeding sick people at the hospital where Mohm had died. "All right," I said softly. "I'll be down in a second." He grabbed the teapot to use as a bowl and we walked slowly to the hospital, our arms interlocked. But when we arrived, it was too late. There was no food for Da. We saw a Khmer Rouge woman scooping rice out for the women in her group and approached her.

"Sister, I'm here to get food," Da said, standing in front of her. She ignored him.

"Please," I begged. "Give my brother just a little food. Have some compassion. You see, our Me-Krum sent him here."

She looked at us with contempt and yelled, "Get out of here! You're not a patient."

Weeping, Da begged, "My Me-Krum told me to come here because I am sick."

"There's no food left. You see?" What we saw was food. She was giving each of the people in her group a plate full of rice. Da's face of sadness looked like the setting sun.

"We are very hungry, Sister," I continued to beg. We saw so much rice falling on the ground! When I stooped to put some in my pocket, she grabbed a bamboo ladle and swung it at my face. It missed me by an inch but smacked Da right on the chest. He managed to stay on his feet. The woman looked very young and too beautiful to be so cruel. She was about to strike again, but I took Da's hand and ran. Our stomachs were filled with hunger and fear. Our hearts were chilled with sadness.

The Old People who had joined the Khmer Rouge revolution in the early years, had the authority to kill animals and catch fish to eat. Sometimes, after all the Old People ate their meals — meals of meat and not just soupy rice porridge — I would collect the bones they'd thrown away for us to gnaw on. I would clean the bones and cook them. Sometimes, I would steal the cow skin they dried in the sun to make into a special rope. I would hide it in the river for a couple of days to soak and then boil it in my teapot.

That evening, after failing to get food for Da at the hospital, I was going to the river to wash myself and saw a big piece of cow skin. I went back to the house and got a knife and when it was dark outside, returned to cut a piece off the hide. It was like eating rubber, but it filled us for the night.

The Khmer Rouge children were cruel to Da. I would never have done such horrible things to other children and told myself I would never become like them. They abused and mocked him, and spat on him in disgust. I hated them with all my heart. Even when he could no longer walk, they made fun of him and tried to make him work. Da waited for death.

One evening, he sat in front of the teapot, stirring water and crying as the children shouted at him. "You go back to work," they taunted. "We've already given you a few days to get better. Maybe you're just too lazy. You're faking your illness. You're lucky we gave you a few days off."

Later that evening, I came home to find Khmer Rouge boys poking and hitting Da's swollen body with a bamboo stick and laughing. He sat there motionless, like a dead person, then tried to inch away. Had they punctured him, he would have died and his suffering would have been over. I just stood there looking in and seeing my only surviving brother in pain and tears. Mother would have thrown herself against these children.

"Please," I said, "leave him alone. Take pity on him. He doesn't want to be sick. Look at his swelling. He can't move. If he could, he would go to the field."

"Don't tell us what to do!" they shouted back. "It's none of your business." Then the evening bell rang and they ran home.

Every day, I walked Da to the hospital for his food and tried to make sure we got there on time. That same woman would stare with hatred at him and sometimes hit him on the head with the ladle before giving him the rice. If I'd had the strength or meanness to kill her, I would have done it then. My brother was suffering so much. Every day, his rice was salted by his own tears.

One evening, Da and I returned from the hospital without any food. We decided to bathe in the river. Birds were flitting from one tree to the next, singing happily. It was just the two of us there in the river. We scrubbed each other's backs with our sorrow, wishing one of the birds overhead could be our dinner. Da said an old man had told him that if he boiled a particular wild grass and drank it, his swelling would go down. But it was dangerous. He could die from diarrhea. Da asked me to help him decide what to do.

"I want to go back to work," he said. "Help me get the swelling down." His body was so heavy now that he had to drag himself inch by inch and the effort only made him weaker. "I am tired," he said. "I want the wild grass. It might help me heal the swelling."

I thought about this decision all night. I didn't want to lose him. But a daily scoop of rice wasn't helping him get better. It couldn't overcome the years of malnutrition and lack of medicine. There was no sign that he would ever get well. Every night, his temperature alternated between fever and chills. When the cold wind blew in off the river, he would shiver like a sick puppy. He often asked me to sit on him to keep his body from shaking.

The next day, when I came back from work, I brought him the grass. I didn't want him to risk death, but I didn't want him to continue to suffer, either. I sat with him in front of the fire. His eyes were lit up by the flame and he was smiling. I hadn't seen him with a happy expression since Mother died.

So I boiled the wild grass in my teapot for Da. The grass turned dark purple. I felt as if I were preparing a poison for my own brother. I had prayed, invoked, and called out to the spirits of our mother, father, and ancestors to aid him.

"Do you really want to do this?" I asked one final time.

"It's OK, don't worry about me," he said.

I gave him two cups of the broth and he gulped them down with great relief. I fell asleep while he lay flat with his eyes open, waiting for the grass to stir his stomach. Over the next few hours, he had constant diarrhea and, true enough, his swelling went down. He became so hungry. He wanted something to eat immediately. He was craving sweets especially. There was no way I could find any kind of food in the middle of the night. I thought how as soon as it was light, I would ask the old woman next door for help.

Meanwhile the diarrhea got so bad that sometimes Da couldn't move fast enough and I had to help him wash himself.

Then, after everything was cleaned out of his system, he could no longer move. He was only bones and skin, and so pale it seemed he did not even have blood anymore. I could see his eye sockets.

"I am so sorry, brother," I said, weeping.

"It's not your fault," he said. "Maybe it's better this way."

"I'll do whatever I can to help you, Da," I promised.

In the morning, the old woman stopped by to take a look at my brother. When she saw his condition, she went back to her place for a cup of rice that I could make into porridge.

"Thank you, thank you, Grandmother," I said, clasping my hands and kneeling in front of her in gratitude. I didn't go to work that day. I didn't care what the Khmer Rouge did to me. Da was so weak. His clothes and blankets smelled and flies were buzzing all around him.

He had become unrecognizable, a skeleton. I laid blankets on the floor to cushion him. It was unbearable to hear the effort of his breathing.

"Keep strong, brother," I said. "Please don't leave me." But he could not speak.

Several hours after I had wiped away his last tears, Da slipped into his death-world of joy, where a feast would be waiting for him. Mother would cook him the greatest meal, and nothing of this earth would linger in his mind. With remorse and guilt, I wrapped him in the blankets that were stained with his own smell and prostrated myself in prayer. As the lonely night came, I sat alone next to Da's body.

"May his life journey be to a better place," I murmured. *"May he always have enough to eat, love to give, and happiness to spread. I will join you soon, my brother."*

All around, there was silence. I was too numb to take his body away. How would I drag him out of the house? How would

I remember him? I didn't even have a picture of him. *"Take him, Mother. Take him back into your arms."*

In the morning, I sat on the steps waiting for assistance. A man came and helped me take Da behind the temple, which had become both a killing ground and a burial place. We dug a grave to fit his pathetic body into, and laid him to rest. I hadn't heard from Chan, Theary or San. I didn't know what happened to them. Maybe they have died or been killed. Nobody except me, I thought, will know that he'd ever lived.

He was my brother and my friend. I was determined to survive and remember him not as a boy who suffered great agonies and pain but as a happy child. I vowed to forgive those who had done him wrong and never to do unkind things to others.

My heart was heavy and my head ached. When I got back from the field that day, I laid my body on the floor and fell asleep. Later on, I heard a voice. It was the old woman who had secretly helped us many times. She had come to tell me I was going to be late for my portion of food. Without hesitation, I grabbed my teapot and ran for that meal. I realized that I was truly alone now, eating with just the spirits of my mother, father, and two brothers around me, smiling their sad smiles. I wished that by magic I could have shriveled away.

The old woman said I could bring my things to her house, which was just a few meters away, and live there until the village leader decided what to do. That night I went to sleep on her front porch. My life had no meaning to me anymore and I thought that maybe if they killed me now I could join the spirits of my family in heaven, with no more suffering.

TEN

River of the Dead

I continued to watch the death all around me. Most people died of starvation, but some died from illnesses because they no longer had any immunity left. Some were executed. Plastic bags were wrapped around their bullet wounds and cracked skulls. During the monsoon season, their rotting bodies came floating up on the flooded plain. Were they someone's husband or wife, mother or father, brother or sister, I thought? Could that be one of my brothers or sisters? They looked like dead fish.

One evening, my Me-Krum said, "You don't belong in this village. You have to go with Comrade Jouk to an orphan mobile team." I thought this was my death sentence.

Jouk turned out to be the guy I had seen beating my brother Da in front of the village leader's house for stealing bamboo shoots. He didn't know I recognized him. I wanted to kill him, but I knew I wasn't strong enough and might die at his hands instead. How many people had he killed? I wondered.

"Met Seng, let's go!" he ordered.

I jumped up as fast as I could and took my mother's teapot, spoon, and bundle. As I trailed behind him, I didn't say a word. He walked in a strange way, like a bird. His black pajamas were full of air and ruffled against his thighs. He held a sickle with a sharp, curved blade and an AK-47 strapped around his shoulder.

On the way to the orphan camp, we stopped to rest under a palm tree. After sticking the sickle into the tree, he slid his gun off and leaned against the trunk. Then he took tobacco from his pocket and rolled himself a cigarette with a leaf. Neither of us said a word. There were no other people around, just me, Jouk, and the slender palm tree. All that time, while he was enjoying his hand-rolled cigarette, I thought about what he might do to me with the sickle or the gun. Or maybe with his hands. Finally, he said something.

"Met Seng," he called my name as if he were calling me to march to a ditch where I'd be shot and left for the vultures.

"Yes, Comrade," I answered humbly, my voice trembling.

"Was your family rich?"

I remembered that we were never to tell anyone about our past. We were poor with no education. "No, Comrade," I said, hiding my face. I stared at the earth and felt the trembling of this answer.

He sat down to caress his gun, smiling as if he knew I was telling a lie.

"Tell me the truth," he pressed. "Do you read and write? If you can, Angkar will assign you to teach children at the mobile team. In fact, Angkar will promote you to a group-leader position."

I didn't know if I could trust him. Those who had admitted to an education before had been taken away to be killed, but he looked serious. Maybe this mobile team was a new way to reeducate the children. Finally I said, "No, Comrade. I was too young to be in school and we were too poor. My mother couldn't afford it."

"Met, you don't look poor," he said. "You have light skin. People like you had it easy in life." He could see through me. What should I say? 'No, we survived by selling junk like Pepsi Cola bottles and cans?' Saying that hadn't saved Father.

But I persisted. I said, "No, my parents collected junk and sold it for a living."

Met Jouk pulled the sickle out of the tree and picked up his gun. I thought he was going to shoot me, but he said, "Let's go, Met."

It was about midday when we arrived at the mobile orphan camp. As far as my eyes could see, there were rice paddies—field after field—so much rice it made me wonder again why we were starving.

At the entrance, Met Jouk told me to wait while he looked for the leader. Other children, just back from the fields, were eating lunch. They all looked exhausted and overworked. Most had light skin. They must be city kids, I thought, whose parents have been killed or starved.

The camp leader was Met Soar, who was about eighteen years old. He was short and had a light complexion and slanted eyes, and walked with his back bent like an old man. Perhaps Met Soar had once been one of the New People and had become Angkar's child. I envied his strength and health. He had the flesh I should have had, round with fat and muscles. I hoped he would be compassionate. I stopped hoping when I saw him beat a child for stealing rice. He had the authority to torture and kill anyone guilty of the smallest crime against Angkar. He had been taught to take orders and control us. The Khmer Rouge came in many shapes and sizes, and their skin might be light or dark, but they were always mean and always found a fault to punish harshly.

That night, Met Soar brought me a straw mat and blanket and showed me to a thatched hut. "Here is your place," he said. I was happy to have the mat and blanket. I felt my family was with me in spirit, following me wherever I went, even into this little sty. There was a roof to keep me dry from the rain and protect me from sun and wind.

After I laid the mat and blanket down, I was given a small bowl of thin rice porridge in the kitchen and sent to the fields, where I was assigned to Group Number Five. It was supposed to be a group for young adults, even though I was very small and only nine years old. I was handed a hoe. Our group had to dig irrigation canals and build small dams in the fields to regulate the flow of water, while the smallest children pulled weeds and the next biggest children plowed and sowed rice. Nobody spoke. There was just the sound of children digging and shoveling, and Met Jouk patrolling with his gun.

That evening, a boy was beaten. We could hear him screaming and begging for it to stop. The sound of the bamboo stick slashing open his body made us cringe.

"Brother, please, I beg of you, please. I didn't steal Angkar's food!" the boy screamed. His head was bleeding and he shook with convulsions. One of the Me-Krums arrived and kicked him in the head as hard as if he were shooting for the goal at a soccer match. The beating was intended to teach us a lesson. *This* is what could happen to us if we went against Angkar. The Khmer Rouge said they were our parents and then they beat us.

They kicked and beat that boy to death, then dragged his body away. He was all bones, so light and scrawny that anybody could have picked him up with one hand. I thought, It's better for him, even though he had to die in pain. His spirit will be remembered. He will be united with his parents and maybe he will keep an eye on all of us. They wrapped his body with a piece of cloth, tied it up, and pulled it up to the dam. I remembered the floating bodies at the village and realized where they'd come from.

"Our Angkar Loeu will not allow such a bad example," the Me-Krum said, referring to the district leader. "We must eliminate all the enemies who complain and steal food from our camp."

I had survived this far because I was quick, silent, and able to steal. In the field, I kept my eyes on things I could eat—insects, worms, mice, lizards, crickets, any crawling creature—and was quick to grab them. When we dug canals, I found roots and water nuts. In the old village, I'd sneak out at night and find things in the dark to put in my mouth and bring back to eat. But after seeing that boy killed at the orphan camp, I had second thoughts—if I was caught, I didn't think I could handle the pain. And I thought no matter how quick or how smart I was, I was sure to be caught one day. But the hunger! What would I do with the hunger?

Angkar owned everything, not just the bamboo but the sky, water, land, and grass. Eyes were watching my every move. The Khmer Rouge always said, "Angkar has many eyes, like a pineapple." Even after all this time I wondered, who was this Angkar? Was he one of them or a god? How could he be a god if they didn't believe in anything religious?

It was dusk. The food bell had rung and everyone brought their bowl and spoon to sit in circles of ten. We had been waiting for this moment all day long. As soon as our Me-Krum set down a pail of hot rice porridge in the middle, everyone began pushing and shoving, elbowing one another to scoop it into their bowls. Everyone else had a big spoon, but mine was very small, so I used my bowl to scoop, putting my hand in the hot boiled rice and filling my bowl before the others. I knew that was cheating, but otherwise I wouldn't get enough with my little spoon. We looked down, away from one another, and sounded like pigs swilling food as we ate. It took only a few minutes for the pail to be licked clean and every grain devoured.

After the meal, we had to go to a meeting. At the meetings, the leaders would drill into us that we were Angkar's children and had to be very strong. "Angkar's children are tough," they said. "They do not speak unless asked, nor do they complain, cry, or get emotional. No one is allowed to talk, sing, play or do whatever they feel like." They seemed to make up new rules as they went along. If they caught us "stealing" anything, even bugs, our hands would be chopped off. Every meeting was the same.

The moon became my enemy because when it was full, we had to work at night. I was angry with the moon when it shone brightly on the earth. The leaders seemed to want us to drop dead from exhaustion. We didn't even learn one another's names. Each night, I crawled into my little pen exhausted and hungry.

One night, a Chinese boy who shared my little thatched barn was caught stealing from the kitchen. To set an example for the others, he was beaten in the middle of the camp. Angkar demanded loyalty through terror, pain, or death. Either a child silently obeyed, after being tortured and mutilated, or died at the hands of sadistic young killers. The Me-Kong grabbed the boy by his hair and screamed, "Thief! You see this boy. He tried to steal when Angkar warns again and again not to steal. All of you, take a good look at his face." The boy tried to make his case by pleading. He cried. In doing so, he had committed triple crimes—stealing, crying, and showing his weakness. As he was being tortured, the rest of us fell silent, and it was as if we'd been shut off from birds, wind, and earth. Everything around us, even the Me-Krum's screaming accusations, was dead.

That night, I had been late, but had managed to sneak into the meeting. When I saw the boy being beaten, I was afraid I would be forced up there with him, my hands tied behind my back, while the others watched as if they were at a play. I thought about how many times I had been lucky—all those times in the old village I could have been caught and killed—and felt again that I had not lived long enough yet. Somehow, somewhere, someday there would be a place to escape to. My mother's spirit must have been watching and protecting me.

Later, I decided to sneak out in search of food to steal. The boy who slept on my left woke up. It was the only time I could freely ask his name. It was Hong. He was thin and tall, with light skin and long fingers. He looked like a praying mantis in his skeletal frame, full of hunger bites that develop on the skin from malnutrition. I told him I was going outside for a second, but he knew what I was going to do and quietly wished me luck and hoped I would bring him some food, too. I didn't find enough that night to even fill myself.

During the rainy season, there was usually a little more to eat. Herbs and edible flowers would sprout, and frogs and small animals would come out in a light rain. Whenever that happened I grabbed whatever came my way. I dug my fingers into the wet earth and pulled out roots. Rice, too, began to grow and flower during the rainy season. The rice flowers were sweet. Rice grew tall and I could hide in it. In the water, I'd catch fish or find snails or little shrimps, which were very good raw.

The rice fields were divided into squares by the dikes we built, and the canals next to them kept the water running from field to field, like our suffering. I heard that the ancient Angkor civilization had been built on this irrigation system, which had produced enough rice to enable it to conquer other lands. Still, there was not enough rice for the camp, and I watched children die of malnutrition, some swollen up like Da, others gaunt like me.

The Khmer Rouge children were told to observe us day and night, and some were allowed to carry out killings. The rules got stricter and stricter. After a while, I could not sneak out as easily at night. For some reason, they let me keep my mother's teakettle; when they asked, I said I used it to boil water.

Angkar was forcing us to work harder and harder. They said that we must speed up rice production. We had to do one project after another, toiling with empty bellies in the rain and the burning heat. The girls worked in one section of the field, while the boys worked in another; plowing, husking, digging, building irrigation dams, pulling weeds, standing, bending, sorting hopes from dreams and horrors from realities. If you stood idle even for a minute, the Me-Krum would come up behind you with a bamboo whip and strike you on the back.

My Me-Krum marked areas of weakened dams for me to patch up. First, I'd loosen some wet earth, swinging my hoe up and down. Then, I'd shove it into a mud basket and, after carrying it to the damaged dam, mix in wild grasses I'd pulled up to make it sturdier. I would do this hour after hour every day.

At the end of the day, I could hardly walk. My stomach had started to eat away my flesh. Then dehydration set in. I had no salt, no ability to taste anything. My skin began to yellow. I was afraid of becoming as sick as Da had been.

I began to hate everything. I hated the rain. I hated the Khmer Rouge. I hated the blue sky., I hated myself and I longed for death. I hated not having my mother, my father, my brothers and sisters. I hated not having a full stomach three times a day. I hated not going to the market with my mother. I hated not having the sweets and the coconut juice. I hated not being in our home, though I doubted it would be the same even if I were to return.

We were working in nonstop rain, far into the night. I would work for eight hours at a time, using all my energy lifting heavy earth to build dams. Some of them would be washed out by rain, so we would have to rebuild them right away, for the pride of Angkar. I didn't know how long I could hold on. The Me-Krum did nothing but walk up and down the dikes, patrolling with his gun and his vulture eyes.

One day, I decided to work slowly to kill time. I pretended to bob my head up and down, and move from side to side as if I was working. Really I was only lifting small amounts of earth. Suddenly my Me-Krum came from behind and put a large black ant on my neck. I jumped and screamed at its sharp bite. The Me-Krum laughed. Then I swore a curse, and he grew angry. "Met Seng, you are still using this city language. You're slacking! Angkar does not like city language. This language of yours is what Angkar has sorely fought against. Don't let me hear it again!" I wanted him dead, but knew my mother wouldn't want me to wish death upon anybody, so instead I hoped one day he would just disappear into the blackness he wore over his heart.

The rain stopped, but there was nothing to cheer about. The Me-Krum had blown his whistle, which meant meeting time, not dinner. I was so afraid I would be subjected to reeducation. We were sitting in rows, thinking of food, when I heard my name. "Met Seng didn't work hard enough today and he used city language. Stand up, Met Seng," he said. My knees were shaking and I called silently in my head out to my mother's spirit to save my life.

"Come and sit in front of everyone," Me-Kong Soar ordered.

"Mother," I prayed, *"I am in danger now. Please help and protect me from these evil Khmer Rouge."*

"Met Seng," the Me-Krum said. "You must work harder tomorrow."

"Yes. Yes. I am very sorry. I will work harder tomorrow. Please forgive me."

He didn't beat me or even scold me. My mother must have convinced him. Then the sky darkened and the rain started to fall again.

The next morning, the bell struck three times and woke us up as usual at five. It was still dark. I rolled up my mat, washed my face, picked up my hoe, and headed down to the field, which was a few miles away.

ELEVEN

My Mother's Spirit

I still managed to sneak out and find food. Sometimes after the meeting, I told my Me-Krum that I was going down the canal to bathe. While I washed I looked for crabs, snails, and fish—there was plenty of food, it was just that the Khmer Rouge didn't allow us to have it. Before I went to sleep, I usually made a fire next to my mat—we were allowed to do this because it was cold—and boiled water in my teakettle on a stone tripod. The snails and crabs would go into the water. I would put some roots into the pot to cover up my snail-and-crab soup and make it seem as if I was boiling a traditional medicinal tea. The Me-Kong and Me-Krum would walk around to see if anybody was cooking food. If they caught us cooking anything, they would take it away and beat us, sometimes to death.

One night, my Me-Krum asked what I was boiling in my teakettle. "Met Seng, what's in the kettle?"

"I'm boiling water, Comrade," I told him.

"Open the lid. I want to see what's in the kettle."

When I opened the lid, he saw the roots and said, "Boiling water, hey? Boiling water! Ha."

"Oh, Comrade," I said, "this is a traditional medicine. I drink it to keep me from swelling and diarrhea so I can work harder for Angkar!"

He glanced into my pot again. My snails and crabs were dead, buried underneath the branches of the phony herbs. Once again, I was spared. It was if my mother's spirit had taken possession of the teapot to keep me alive. I ate my delicacies quietly under my blanket, where no one would know except Hong. He was quick to hear me chewing.

"What are you eating? Can I have some?" he begged.

"No. I don't have any more food. I ate it all," I told him through a mouthful of crabs. But he begged and begged until finally I gave him a crab. For many other boys, it was already too late. They should have taken a chance and gone out to look for food like I did. But maybe they didn't have a teapot like mine.

Hong and I became good buddies over that crab. We decided to trust each other and always to cover for each other. After that, whenever I had food, I shared it with him. Hong was too afraid to look for food himself. I decided to share everything I caught with him so that he might live as long as me. It was nice to finally have a friend I could trust.

One morning at the end of the rainy season, the work bell rang. Hong was usually awake before me, but that morning I didn't see him. After I went to wash my face, I went to his mat to see if he was still asleep, and there he was, rolled up like a ball, all f rozen stiff.

"Hong, didn't you hear the bell has rung?" I said. "Wake up! We have to go to work."

There was nothing but silence. I shook him again and again, then pulled the blanket off and found his body was rigid and cold. The crab I'd given him the night before was his last taste of life. If I hadn't given it to him, I wouldn't have been able to face his death.

He died knowing that there were good people left in the world. He was so lonely, so hungry, so full of desire for life. I went to tell the Me-Krum.

"Hong died last night," I said.

"You go and take him away," he responded, as if Hong had been just a dog. He told another boy to help me take Hong somewhere to be dumped.

I put a false look of dedication to Angkar on my face. "Met, where do I take the body?"

"Anywhere," he said. "Anywhere you can find a spot. Just dump him there. When you finish with that, come to meet the group at Zone One near the highway."

I wrapped my dead friend in his cotton blanket and carried him to a dry spot. I didn't want to leave him exposed, but there was no spot for us to dig. I listened to Hong's spirit and decided to throw him into one of the canals so that he could float downstream with the rest of the dead, wherever the water might take them. I let him go into the strong current, with the hope that someone downstream would bury him.

Sometimes I would daydream while I was working in the field. When I saw a bird, I wanted to be like him, flying in the sky, free of all the suffering around me. I remembered one time when I was very little and Mother took me on an airplane from Phnom Penh to Kampot, where she had grown up. The trip took about an hour. It had seemed such a long ride, and how neatly arranged our land looked, seen from above. I imagined that was what birds saw when they flew over us while we were working.

There was more and more death. Most of the children were dying of starvation. And new city kids would arrive every few days. Some caught malaria and other diseases caused by malnourishment. At night, I dreamed. *Dead bodies were floating on the water. Hong, wrapped in the white cloth, had landed on a shore with other bodies that included my brothers and sisters and parents. Their eyes were popping out like fish eyes. Their mouths gaped open. I looked out into the fields and there was nothing but bodies. No rice. No green fields.*

I didn't scream. I just woke up, biting on my tongue.

I looked very sickly now. My skin was yellowed and my body had swelled up. The most common causes of death were swelling, diarrhea, and malaria, but the children in my group also got strange infections from working in the sun, rain, water and mud. Our food was often dirty and cold. Sometimes it was mixed with bindweeds, normally fed to pigs. Flies were always buzzing around us. The water wasn't clean and it gave us diarrhea. Angkar said we could not complain. I craved the dessert my mother used to make— powdered cookies stuffed with sesame seeds and sweet beans, fried in a big wok. We ate these during New Year. I also missed the palm juice Mother used to buy for me whenever we went to the market.

I boiled my drinking water and sometimes put herbal roots in it for flavor and the swelling came and went. Sometimes I felt as if I had put on tons of weight overnight. Whenever I puffed up, I moved slowly. I began to know what Da had gone through when his body looked like a balloon filled with water. Some days, I couldn't feel my own legs or face. My swollen eyelids blurred my vision. I would have been scared to see myself in a mirror.

TWELVE

In the Embrace of Angkar

One morning a district leader came with a group of Kong Chlops on horses. The work bell had rung and the Me-Krum walked from one barn sty to the next calling us all to a meeting. His blood-curdling voice made our hearts stop. We gathered and waited for instruction. All around us were Kong Chlops with American M16 rifles or Chinese AK-47 rifles strapped around their shoulders, hanging loose to their knees. They looked at us as if we were their enemies from another life. Their eyes held us hostage. As the head district leader began to speak, we pretended to applaud, but our weak hands were screaming for mercy. We didn't care about Angkar. All we wanted was food. The leader informed us that Angkar wanted us to start a new project. The rice had not grown as well as expected in Tuk Chjo Village, so we would go there to work.

"Weeds and wild grass," he screamed over the megaphone, "are taking over our rice fields! Today, you all will stay in the temple and work around the village." It was the temple where my father had been murdered.

We chanted slogans to show that we were enthusiastically dedicated to their revolution. *"Chey yo, chey yo, Padavath Kampuchea! Chey yo! Kong Komar Chean Mouk, Moha Os Cha!"* Angkar's children, youth of the Great Leap Forward, revolutionary pioneers of tomorrow. "Chey yo! Chey yo!"

After our rice porridge—by now this porridge had little or no rice in it, sometimes just boiled water with a few grains—we started back to Tuk Chjo, the place where we'd begun this dark part of our lives. All of the children in my group had lost their parents there.

It was not the same road that Comrade Jouk and I had traveled on. This road was much narrower and was connected in places with the interprovincial highway. Hundreds of us walked onward with our few belongings . . . a mournful parade of slow-moving, swollen skeletons.

I daydreamed about which way I would go after if we were finally freed. I didn't think I could ever find my way back to our home in Kampong Speu. But if I didn't, how would I tell my other brothers and sister who were separated from us when the Khmer Rouge took over, when they were living in the city, if they survived, where to find me? I thought about my mother. She would have been happy to hear that I was returning home. If only they'd given her enough to eat, we would have been more than happy to work, and live, and maybe everything would have been different. Mother would have been OK and would be waiting for me with some food already prepared.

Back in Tuk Chjo Village, I went to the riverside to wash up. I remembered where Da and I had buried Mother—I'd marked the spot in my mind—and the exact time of day. I knew I was glad to still be alive, even in the midst of horrors and deprivation.

At the temple we were joined by about fifty city children from another mobile team. Together, there were more than a hundred children still alive. We'd had a common experience. We'd been witnesses to killings, victims of beatings and senseless sicknesses. The temple made me think about a time in the distant past when Cambodians followed a religion of compassion and love. They erected statues in Buddha's likeness and wrapped garlands around his shoulders. They robed him with divine cloths. For so many years, there had been people who'd tried to be good human beings, who respected all living creatures—even little creatures made the world go 'round. But where were these people now? What happened to them? Had they all been killed, even the monks?

Once, temples like this had been filled with chants and holy music, the sounds of gongs and bells. You could hear the laughter of children running with glee as they celebrated the New Year. In Kampong Speu, Mother would dress in her best traditional clothes to bring Buddha the offering of her labor. The monks would feast on what they received. There was no war, no violence or torture.

"Angkar Leu (the High Organization) is coming!" the leader shouted, pulling me out of my memory. We were ordered to go to the highway and wait for the arrival of the great revolutionary leader. Everyone in the village had to assemble and greet him. This was exciting because it meant that we wouldn't have to work. They told all the Old People who looked healthy and strong to work close to the highway so that Angkar Leu would see that everything was going well. The New People were all to work behind, hidden. We were the skinny, unhealthy-looking ones, with our swollen bodies. Soldiers made sure we didn't run out in protest to show this Angkar that we were dying of starvation and slave labor. Not that we would have dared to do such a thing.

Around midday, military jeeps with red flags arrived. They were filled with Chinese officials. I learned years later that the Khmer Rouge had imported the Great Leap Forward plan from China. Maybe all the rice we produced was going to feed the over-populated masses there.

I worked from dawn to dusk, twelve hours or more a day, without a break or lunch. I sometimes pretended to labor hard, but my real work was looking for baby mice. One morning, I found a bunch of them in a hole. I grabbed them and hid them in my black pants. When I got home, I cooked them in my teapot. These little mice were very tender because they'd just come from their mother's belly. I boiled them in my pot. The other children were envious. Some begged me to share, but I was no longer willing to share. I knew I had to take care of myself or die. I had to survive and I would eat whatever I could get my hands on. Those children had to be smart and find their own meals. I ate everything, because leftovers would have been stolen by the next morning. If I'd had to, I think I would have eaten a human being.

Life got a little better in November as the harvest approached. I dreamed of bowls filled with white rice and curried chicken. I stayed alive hoping the Khmer Rouge would give us enough to eat. Now I received only a spoonful of rice every day. But it was enough to bring down my swelling.

It was pleasantly cool in December, our winter. The wonderful dry breeze caressed my face. One day I looked up and saw that the sky was clear and blue. The weather was just perfect. It was not too cold or too hot. Somehow, things looked beautiful and hopeful across the rice-covered landscape. I imagined myself in the middle of it, calling out to my mother who was husking rice. We were peasants, but not prisoners, working in these fields, growing the rice city people buy for their daily meals.

Such interludes never lasted long. As soon as the harvest season began, we had to work extra hard to collect rice and pick up every grain that fell to the ground during threshing. The Kong Chlops (Spies) and other Khmer Rouge soldiers would check our pockets and search our bodies every time we left the field.

One morning it was my turn to sweep the temple grounds. It was around midmorning when I finished and started to walk down to the field to look for my group. But there was no one around. I kept looking and searching for everyone. I couldn't understand where my group had gone. Suddenly, I was alone, with a whole world of rice fields, one after another, to myself. I bent down and crawled on my knees into one of the rice paddies. I crouched down and started to harvest the rice with my hand, pulling and squeezing the grain a handful at a time onto my checkered red *krama*. I also put some into my pockets. When I had gotten all this rice, I couldn't figure out how to take it into the temple without being seen or caught. I was so happy at the thought of having it for dinner, but they would surely catch me if I were searched. For a few minutes, I sat there hidden in the tall golden rice, thinking and wondering whether it was worth the risk. As I sat quietly thinking, a stone smashed into my shoulder. "Who's in there?" A voice called for me to come out. I knew I had been caught. Then I realized that there were two people there.

"Get out now! Don't think that you're going to get away," they both yelled. There were two Kong Chlops, wanting me dead. My knees trembled as I stood up. I was shaking at the thought of being beaten and killed on the spot. Again, I called to the spirits of my parents. This time I was in real danger.

"Met, get over here quickly!" one of the Kong Chlops shouted. "Met, kneel and take the rice out of your pockets." I started to empty my pockets for them.

"What's in the *krama*?" the other one asked.

"Rice, Comrade," I told them. They started to laugh.

"Untie it and empty everything on the ground."

"Yes, Met." My hands were shaking. One of the Kong Chlops kicked me from behind. I fell on my face.

"Didn't we tell you again and again not to steal from Angkar? Who told you to steal?" One of them kicked me again. I couldn't answer because I was in pain.

"No one told me to do it, Comrade. I did it of my own free will. I was hungry."

Then they cut some vines with which to tie my hands behind my back and pushed me up the side of a ditch for further interrogation.

"Met, tell me the truth. How many times have you stolen Angkar's rice?

"This is my first time stealing, Comrade. Please, don't hurt me! I am sorry! Honest!"

"First time? Ha! This is your first time, huh?" The two of them began kicking me until my body was all bruised. My nose and my mouth were bleeding. I felt so dizzy. Everything started to spin. With my hands tied to my back, I easily lost balance and fell flat on my face. I said softly in shaky voice "Mother, please help me!" I cried. "Comrades, don't kill me!" I begged. They kept beating me until I fell down into a small canal. I struggled to get up, but one of them grabbed me by the hair and pushed my face into the water. I fought and struggled to breathe.

"This is what you get for stealing from Angkar. Doesn't Angkar feed you enough?"

Finally, after they pushed and pulled my head in and out of the water, one of them decided that I should be put in front of the village leader. With my hands still tied, they ordered me to follow them. They zigzagged purposely to make me lose my strength.

They took me to a shady place under some palm trees and propped me in front of a group of Khmer Rouge children. They were squatting in the shade smoking cigarettes. None of them were from my mobile camp or Tuk Chjo Village. But one of them reminded me of Jouk. And he was to be my judge.

"Met, we caught this thief stealing rice," one of the Kong Chlops said. "Do you know him? Does he belong to your camp?"

"No, but leave him here. We can take care of him," said the judge. The two Kong Chlops left, but the torture was not over yet. Still with my hands tied behind my back, I squatted in the circle of Khmer Rouge children. One of them came up to me with a bamboo stick, then poked me in the ear and laughed.

"Look at his big ears. They look like elephant ears," he taunted. The other children started to laugh and kick me. I fell flat and at that moment, a hard kick came from behind my head. They left me there for dead. I must have blacked out.

When I came to, everything was still, as if no one existed but me. It was late afternoon and the sun was about to set. I must have been lying there for several hours. I looked around and saw nothing except birds eating rice from the field. I was struggling to untie my hands, but my skin was cracked and the bruises from the beating scared me. There was blood mixed with mud all over my body. Again, I felt I must have been saved by the grace of my mother's protection. She must have been watching. I'd been lying as though dead on the ground for several hours. Suddenly I saw a woman walking toward me, and when I called for help she quickly came to my rescue. She was one of the New People.

"Sister, please help me."

"What happened to you?" she asked.

"Please, untie me." The woman looked around to see if there were any Khmer Rouge in the area. Just because it was quiet, it didn't mean they weren't watching. She untied me and said, "Go, run away from here. Go as fast as you can." I didn't know her name. I didn't even get a chance to say thank you.

My body ached everywhere. I could hardly walk, but I finally returned to the temple where my group was. Now I had to think of some excuses for why I had been absent from work the whole day. I went to the river to wash up. My face and body were bruised and bloody. My clothes were all torn. What was I going to say to my Me-Krum?

That evening, when I went to get my spoonful of rice, my Me-Krum didn't say a word. There were so many children under his control that he must not have even missed me. I felt so relieved. After my meal, I went to sleep with my pain and tears, calling to my mother for assistance. Somehow, thinking of her helped me forget the pain. I slept through the night and in the morning, it was work as usual. My face was all swollen, but nobody had noticed.

THIRTEEN

The Agony

My friend was not so lucky. He was related to the royal family, he said, and I didn't believe him at first. But his name, Sisovatha, sounded like royalty—one of our kings had been named Sisovath—so that when he told me his name I thought he might truly be related to the royal family. He had a light complexion. He'd never worked a day in his life, he said. He'd had maids to serve him. I imagined that he had never been far outside of the palace. It was possible that he wasn't one of the important royals. He just had the blood. He could have been the son of the king's twentieth wife. I was told that kings could have lots of wives and concubines.

One day, the Khmer Rouge singled out Sisovatha for public torture. He was about fourteen years old. It was in the middle of the day, while we were sitting in a circle having our meal. The secretive Me-Kong who in was charge of our camp, walking side by side with the Kong Chlops, told Sisovatha to walk toward the swamp. I was suddenly unable to swallow my food because I knew what they were going to do to him.

"What did I do wrong?" Sisovatha asked. He resisted going into the dirty water, which was full of leeches. Then one of the Kong Chlops pulled out his gun and aimed at Sisovatha's back. "If you don't go in, then we'll just have to shoot you," he said.

All the other children rushed out from the temple to get a closer look. It was like a gruesome circus show, a deadly festival. We had seen it all before. Sisovatha started walking toward the deep swamp. "We'll tell you when to stop," they told him. "Now, put your hands on your head." Then they said, "Tell us the truth, Met Sisovatha. Did you take a bucket of rice from the field early this morning or not?"

"No, Comrade. I did not take it."

"But I saw you run and duck yourself in hiding this morning," said the Kong Chlop. "I recognized you very well."

"If you don't tell the truth, you will have to stay in the swamp until you die," said the Me-Kong. "Now, tell us, how many times have you stolen rice from Angkar?"

Sisovatha didn't say anything. I wished he would just tell them what they wanted to hear. Then they would have shot him immediately, ending his hell on earth. Instead, the Kong Chlop took big rocks and threw them at Sisovatha until his head was cracked and bleeding. Sisovatha just stood there with his hands on his head feeling his own blood.

"Angkar has lost buckets of rice every night from the storage house and in the field," said the Me-Kong. "Now we know who the culprit is."

"How many times have you stolen the rice?" the Me-Kong screamed.

"Tell us the truth now! Then we'll let you out of the swamp."

Finally, Sisovatha surrendered. "Comrade, I stole rice only one time. That's all."

When he heard that, the Me-Kong went to get a burning log from the temple kitchen and told Sisovatha to come up from the swamp. He thought he was free, but the Me-Kong put the burning log in his hands and told him to hold it. Sisovatha held it for a few seconds and then dropped it. I wanted to help, but there was nothing I could do. Sisovatha ran back to the water to soak his hands. Then, when he came back up, the Kong Chlop started hitting him with his rifle. He made Sisovatha hold the red-hot log again, and ordered him back into the swamp.

"You will be dead if you throw that log down again," he said.

I could see Sisovatha's hands shaking as the log burned through his skin.

"Keep your hands over your head and hold it," they told him. Sisovatha had to hold it until the log burned out. He was screaming, and the Khmer Rouge urged him to scream louder.

"Go ahead, scream as loud as you can. Your dead parents can't help you now. They won't rescue you." They laughed. It was a long time, perhaps half an hour, before the log burned out.

When Sisovatha finally was able to, he stumbled out of the water. I saw that leeches covered his whole body and were hungry for his blood. He can't have much blood left in him, I thought. He was only skin and bone. The leeches clung on to him, sucking away his life. His hands were badly burned, so he couldn't peel or rub the leeches off. He collapsed on the ground.

"This is your first lesson for stealing rice from Angkar," the Khmer Rouge shouted. "If we catch you stealing next time, Angkar will not forgive you."

"Everyone get back to the field and work," the Me-Kong yelled.

Once the Me-Kong and Kong Chlops were done torturing Sisovatha, they left to the fields, I sneaked over quickly before going back to work. I took some sand and rubbed the leeches off of Sisovatha. I couldn't believe that he had survived.

Sisovatha once told me that he never wanted to die with an empty stomach. He didn't care what they did to him as long as he had something to eat. That was why he had stolen the rice. In his royal life, he'd had servants to bring whatever he needed or wanted.

His family was well respected, he said. Now, knowing that he would be killed, he took risks all the time, whatever it took to fill himself up each night before he went to sleep. All his family was gone, and he wanted to die and be with them. He had been tortured in other places many times before. He knew how to endure it. From his body, I could see the scars of those previous tortures. I saw that several of his fingers had been chopped off.

A week later, I woke up and saw that Sisovatha's right leg was badly bruised and swollen. He was lying flat on his face, unable to move his leg, his face puffed up like a blowfish. I told him I wished I could help, but had to go to work. He had to work, too, but he couldn't walk. I knew that something awful would happen to him. When I returned, he was gone. I heard they had buried him alive. He was no longer useful.

Our mobile team had to go from one project to the next. When the work around the old village was done, they told us we were moving to another place, a city. Maybe it was near Kampong Speu, I thought, where I was born. They said only that we were heading east. Just follow the rising sun. That was east.

I thought about Sisovatha, how he must have died in great pain. I wondered sometimes if the soul would ever go somewhere better than this place. I knew that my mother was somewhere, floating around, watching. She had left me in a dangerous situation, so her soul's mission was not yet complete. She could not go on, perhaps, until she knew that I was safe. But why did Sisovatha die? Why didn't his mother protect him as mine had protected me? Maybe it was different for royal families, I thought.

FOURTEEN

The Rope Tighten

As time went on, the Khmer Rouge successfully brainwashed some of the city children and promoted them to group leaders. Met Soar was put in charge of everyone in our mobile camp. He taught us to believe in the miracles of Angkar, how we should dedicate our lives to the good of the community and the goals set forth by the top leaders to create a new Cambodia. I didn't know what he was talking about. When Met Soar told us to spy on our family and friends, I resolved that I would never obey him. Nothing he could say or do would make me betray my family and friends. They had already taken my family, but they would never take my soul and mind. I thought to myself: "your Angkar destroyed my family. No matter how much 'education' you try to influence me with, I am determined that I will never be one of you." What they did was completely wrong to do to any human being.

But I pretended to believe in everything Soar said. When he said, "Be proud of Angkar!" I shouted, "Chey yo, chey yo, Angkar! Glory to Angkar!" We raised our stick like hands and moved our dry lips to stay alive. "We must destroy all forms of religion and social inequality," they said. Every evening, they pounded our brains with the rhetoric of the revolution. We sang songs in praise of Angkar; people were asked to testify in favor of Angkar. We had to stand up one by one to tell others what we had done for Angkar that day. It was like a game, but it wasn't a fun one to play.

"I will work harder for Angkar," I said. "I am committed to take any work assignment and follow any direction Angkar provides."

There was no smile on anyone's face. We were all too exhausted, too weak to show emotion. It took whatever energy I had left, after a long day's work without food, to raise my voice so that everyone could hear my short speech showing my commitment to Angkar. I could feel the eyes of the other children on me. Their applause was loud and chilling. The leaders were watching everybody. The children sat in fear. No one could protest the dogma of Angkar, not even the starving. These little speeches kept us alive. Those who gave the best recitations were rewarded and used as examples.

Many, many children were brainwashed. One night, one of the New People, Rom, was named by Soar as a true child of Angkar. Rom never stole food from Angkar. He endured hunger without complaint. He worked diligently. The leaders raised his status to a Kong Chlop who would watch over Angkar's rice. Anyone caught stealing would answer to Rom. The district leader, Angkar Loeu, congratulated him and we looked upon him with new fear. "Angkar has many eyes," the Angkar Loeu said. "Whoever Angkar trusts the most will be rewarded." He smiled after his address, and Soar gave a speech reminding us why we should be like Rom, who was given new black clothes, a red-checked *krama,* and a pair of sandals made from the tire of a car. Rom was proud of his new status and I could tell he would do just about anything to preserve it. He would kill us if we dared to go against Angkar. All of his innocence was suddenly gone, his conscience destroyed by his power.

Some other city children wanted that power, too. They wanted to be the child Angkar loved so that they could be well fed. A boy named Meng turned his own cousin in for stealing rice. His cousin was taken away and never seen again, and Meng was made a Kong Chlop by the Angkar Loeu to spy on any New People stealing and running away rom Angkar. When I last saw him, he was riding a horse with an AK-47 as his reward.

I kept silent and endured my captivity, waiting for the day I'd be free again. I could never love Angkar after what he did to my parents, brothers, and sisters. I would rather die than become his true child. Never would I discard the love and compassion I had learned from my parents. I believed all these people would go to the hell described on my mother's temple's walls, a place where bad people were boiled, trampled on, and tortured, and where their acts of evil would haunt them. For every suffering they caused, twice as much suffering would return to them.

Some of the children were horribly mean because they followed what the Old People told them to do. All the Old People had to do was to feed a child well and he would do anything they said. I remember how one of these children was made to torture his own mother, who had been caught stealing rice. First he made her empty all her pockets. Then he took a shovel and hit her with it. She knelt before her son, to whom she had given birth and nursed in her gentle arms, and begged forgiveness. But for the son, it was his welcome into Angkar's elite. He screamed, as if spitting in his own mother's face, "I am not your son. I am a son of Angkar!" The mother's heart must have broke at that very moment. He didn't have to kill her. His denial alone did it for him. She collapsed and died right then. To make sure she was really dead, the son took the shovel and drove it deep into her chest. I learned from then on never to trust anyone around me.

Angkar's way of breeding revolutionary successors was with mass weddings. The brides and grooms didn't know each other. Angkar had arranged each marriage. There were hundreds of them from nearby villages waiting in black clothes for the match of their lives. It was grand! All the New People and Old People were invited. Loudspeakers in the trees played revolutionary songs instead of traditional wedding music. On the day of one of these ceremonies, I decided to run away with Darin, one of the boys in my group. We wanted to go to District Three because we had heard that there was more to eat there. The wedding celebration had brought in a very large crowd, and this was a good opportunity to sneak out, since everyone would be too busy to spy on us.

"Darin, let's go," I whispered to him. "If we are going to leave, we must do it now. The Kong Chlops and the Me-Kong won't be looking for us."

Darin and I snuck out and walked past several mass graves in the fields near Ta Pund village, a few miles from Tuk Chjo. By now, we were so used to seeing dead people that we weren't afraid. There were skulls and bones everywhere. Some people had recently been killed and the stench was horrible. Beyond the bodies there was rice in abundance, enough to bring all those dead people back to life.

Darin and I didn't know where we were going. We just kept walking toward the mountains and District Three, where we had heard there was some food. The tall rice hid us and we thought the Kong Chlops wouldn't be able to see us. We were so happy as we walked, filling our shirt pockets with rice. It was a free-for-all. But out of nowhere, there was a Kong Chlop. I recognized this one.

"Darin, we are in big trouble." I shivered. The Kong Chlop had seen us and was walking straight toward us. "He's the boy they brainwashed to kill his own mother."

"We're dead, then," said Darin. He was just as scared as I was.

"Met, where are you going?" At first, we didn't answer because we were too afraid.

"Angkar gives us a day off and we were just taking a walk," I said.

"Met, let me see what's in your pockets," he said.

"Ah…it's rice, Comrade," I said. Then he whipped me on the shoulder with his stick.

"Go over there," he directed. He seemed ready to kill us on the spot. We were walking ahead of him. Next I heard BANG!—a hard hit on Darin's head.

"Aiii!" he screamed. He began to cry.

I knew the next strike would be on my head. I prepared to die. The second strike missed my head and landed on Darin's head again. He covered his head with his hands and turned in the direction of the strike. As he turned, I glimpsed his face, which was red with blood. He was shaky and begging the Kong Chlop to spare his life. He was in tears and fell down, still trying to protect his head. Blood was dripping over his face.

I turned and the Kong Chlop whipped his bamboo stick around. A blow landed squarely on my head. I blacked out a few seconds and felt a ringing in my head. I thought I would not live. Then, after a second hit, I felt numb all over. My legs became weak. For a second I lost my balance, but I didn't fall. I could not hear what the Kong Chlop was saying, but I managed to straighten my back and continue walking forward. My whole body was shaking and I felt sweat pouring down my face. The Kong Chlop was walking behind me; I kept turning around to face him all the time to see if he was going to strike me again. I put my hands over my head to protect my skull. I was so scared that I urinated and defecated in my pants. Again, I called out to my mother to comfort me. Then the Kong Chlop started to whip my left leg, gashing it open. He said he was taking me and Darin to a labor camp nearby, as we followed the dikes in the middle of the rice field.

"Don't try to go anywhere without Angkar's permission," he ordered. Before we arrived he let us clean ourselves in the canal. He'd taken us to an adult labor camp. Darin continued to walk in front of me, holding his head as blood dripped over his face. I thought the Kong Chlop was going to kill me with his own hands. But I also figured if he wanted to kill us, he would have done it already, while we were alone, and then dumped our bodies in the rice field. He said he was going to first get lunch before informing the camp leader what we had done. He tied us up outside the kitchen. with weeds from the rice fields. I could smell the food and my stomach was growling. I wanted what the camp leader was eating so badly. Darin and I waited in the sun, tossing our heads to shoo the flies from our faces.

Then I saw a skinny-looking girl with a *krama* wrapped around her head, watching me. She came to take a closer look at me. She stood right in front of me, but kept her distance. She blocked the sun from my face so she could see who I was. She kept looking at me, smiling.

Finally, she asked, "Are you Seng?"

"Yes," I said, startled.

"I am your sister, Theary!" she said.

"Sister? Theary? Theary!" She untied us. I was so excited that I grabbed her and hugged her. I knew I smelled really bad because I had peed and shat in my pants, but for a moment, I was so happy to know that I still had somebody left in my family. It had been almost three years since I had lost mother, father, and brothers. I wasn't alone anymore.

"What are you doing here?" she asked.

"I got caught by the Kong Chlop. He brought us here," I told her. Darin stood in awe of our coincidental meeting. Suddenly, afraid that one of Kong Chlops would see us, my sister backed away. Then she told us to run away.

"Go! Go! Go! Me-Kong will come out any minute and you will be in big trouble," she said. She ran to the kitchen to see if the leader was still eating his lunch. Then she signaled to us to run. I didn't have a chance to say good-bye or tell her what had happened to Mother, Father, Reth, and Da. At least I knew that someone in my family was alive and one day, if we survived, we would find each other again.

Darin and I ran quickly out of the camp and headed back in the direction of the old village of Tuk Chjo. We came to a stream and I remembered that I couldn't swim. The stream was very deep and the current strong. Darin couldn't swim either.

"But we have to do it, quickly!" Darin said. "We have to take the chance. Ready? Jump!" We kicked and struggled to keep ourselves afloat. I nearly drowned. But we made it across and hid in the rice paddies. Darin and I separated and I went to the river to wash. My body was drained of energy. My head felt so heavy and my face felt like it was full of air. That night, I forgot all about eating. I didn't go for my rice portion because I was afraid other kids would ask me what had happened and my Me-Krom would find out. I fell asleep as soon as I got back to our mobile camp at the temple in Tuk Chjo village. I lay on the floor, and was very sick for a couple of days. I wanted somebody to hold me, maybe sing me a song or give me some candies to bite on. I craved salt. I craved palm juice. Then our mobile team moved from the temple in Tuk Chjo to another camp out in the open fields a few miles from the village.

A couple of weeks later, I went back to the camp where I had met my sister. I found out that she was part of a mobile team, too. They had moved her elsewhere to another project. I kept thinking of her, hoping that she would return to that village. I wanted to find her again. She had given back to me my hope and strength.

FIFTEEN

The Storage Room

Hunger is worse than torture. You get dizzy. You cannot think clearly. Everything gets fuzzy. Your flesh gets thinner and thinner. Soon, you're all bones. All the fat in your body is eaten away or used up by hard work. You never, ever stop thinking about food and where to find some. They warned us, again and again, not to steal from Angkar, but just like Sisovatha, I didn't care. The possibility of being caught was constantly on my mind as I stole from Angkar the rice I had worked hard to produce. It should have been mine to eat anyway.

Angkar assigned more Kong Chlops to patrol the fields at night. They alerted everybody that food was missing from the fields and in the garden. If they caught anyone stealing, there would be no forgiveness anymore. They would kill that person right away. They used torture and public execution to scare us, but we kept stealing. It was at about this time that Rom was made a leader, . He informed on me. Up until then, he had worked hard and never complained and never went to steal food. I used to share the food I stole to shut him up. But when he was made into a Kong Chlop, he turned me in as his enemy.

Almost every night, I would sneak out to the rice paddies. It was dark. That night a gunshot rang out. At the sound of it, I heard children running from the rice fields. There were so many of them—and I'd thought I was alone. I stood there, wondering which way I was supposed to run. Then a voice from behind me yelled out, before I got a chance to flee, "Don't run or I'll shoot! Raise your hands in the air!" I turned to the side and there was one of the Kong Chlops, pointing a gun at me.

"Now move up," he said. "This time you're going to die." I began walking slowly, straight ahead on the dike toward an open space.

"So, this is why Angkar keeps losing rice from the field," he said.

I felt so empty and numb, with chills down my spine. He could have pulled the trigger at any time. Again, I was so terrified that I urinated in my pants. In the open field, about ten other Kong Chlops surrounded me. One of them was Rom. When I saw him, I was happy because I thought he was going to free me. We were neighbors. I had shared my food with him. He'll let me go, I thought. But his eyes cut right through me. He spat in my face and called me the master of thieves. I have to admit that I was very skillful. I had survived all that time by stealing, and if he hadn't informed on me, I would still be the master.

I spoke softly to him. "Comrade Rom, we are friends, remember?"

"You think I would let you go?" He laughed. "You will go to hell, that's where you belong." That meant death. I was frightened and started to cry. The stars above me were so far away. I wished they would fall on these men to take them away. *"Mother,"* I prayed, *"if you're watching, please help me because I am going to die. They are going to kill me."*

Comrade Rom untied a very long rope from his waist and

tied my hands behind my back. Then he tied up other people he had caught that night, one by one, behind me. I thought this would surely be the last night of my life. I could feel my spirit seeking its reunion with my mother, father, and Da in heaven. I thought of Theary and wished to say a last good-bye before they killed me. They would certainly kill me. I was about ten years old and one of the smallest at the mobile camp. I was put in the front of a chain of about twenty thieves who had been too hungry to lie still and sleep. We were tied by a single rope, by our hunger, and by our suffering. They marched us to the temple and locked us up in a dark storage room under the stairway of the chanting hall, an open area inside the building where people used to sit and pray with their hands folded together. They shoved us into that storage room and piled us on top of one another. I was squeezed into the back corner, which was so crowded I could hardly breathe. I could smell my own urine. Rom and his associates left us there and went out in search of more thieves.

We all thought that they were going to execute us that night. Everyone was panicking and struggling to untie their hands. I seemed to be the youngest among them. The rope was so tight that we couldn't free ourselves. Then one man told everyone to be quiet. He said that the Kong Chlops would hear us. He had a small army knife and somehow managed to get it out of his pocket and began to cut the rope.

"Please, quickly! Cut me loose," I told him. I was so anxious to survive and stay alive. Once a new person was cut free, we helped untie the others. And what luck! The door was made of wood. With our collective effort, we pushed the door open. Without any delay or thought, we just ran out of there. It didn't matter where we ended up as long as it wasn't back with the executioners. Where should I go? I wondered. It was almost midnight. The children were sound asleep. I will die no matter what, I thought, at the hands of Rom. No matter where I run to, he will know where to find me.

Instead of going back to my usual sleeping spot, I went to sleep with the dead, in the place in the temple where the bones and ashes of the dead were stored. The Khmer Rouge hadn't yet destroyed this temple. I saw some skulls and bones, but they didn't scare me. I couldn't go to sleep. All I could think of was my own death. For an hour or so, I kept murmuring to myself, invoking Mother's spirit, calling Da, Father, ancestors, and anyone I could think of. I knew they would understand my situation and would do whatever they could to help me. Crying, I prayed to Buddha. Around midnight, I calmed myself down and went back to my hut. But I grabbed my blanket and moved it slightly away from my usual spot. The other children were all asleep. Comrade Rom never came. The next day I went to work as usual, and afterward I went to visit my parents' burial ground and thanked them for helping me.

I hardly saw Rom after that. I made no further attempts to steal food. Instead, I ate throwaway stuff, like fish bones and whatever scraps I could find. We were fed the watery rice gruel with no salt like always, one cup of boiled rice shared by a hundred of us. We were reduced to bone. In my belly, there was more water than rice. I would hear and feel it move as I walked.

Angkar had ordered that we must produce more rice in the rainy and dry seasons. They wanted us to dig water irrigation ditches to store water when the rainy season stopped. The Me-Kongs and Me-Krums insisted that we work harder. Sometimes, as an incentive, they scooped a ladle of rice gruel and distributed it at the work site among those of us who had worked extra-hard. When I could not pick up a hoe or a shovel to dig the dirt, I pushed myself just to make the motion of lifting it so that they could see that I was working. Sometimes I thought I would drop dead. The Me-Krums ordered us to work from dawn until late evening. When the moon was out, our Me-Krum wouldn't waste any time. By the sound of their whistle, we had to get up and stay in the field until they blew their whistle again. We received only one ladle of rice gruel for the whole day.

One night the village leader called a big meeting for all the New People, which included all the children. Our Angkar Loeu, or district leader, informed us that the Vietnamese were coming and anyone attempting to escape would be shot on the spot. We thought of the Vietnamese as our saviors. I prayed for them to liberate us from all the torture. I felt my time running out. It was already the end of harvest time and we were working day and night with almost no food. After the whistle blew, I dug dirt to make a pond or an irrigation canal. We didn't stop working until midnight or later. I was so exhausted that I didn't even wash before bed; I slept with dirt and mud on my body.

One morning, I found I could no longer move. My body was so weak. I decided not to go to the field. Like the others I had seen, I believed I would fall dead on my way to work. My Me-Krum, however, kept blowing his whistle to get me up, but I did not stir. For a moment, I was aware that all the children had gone to the fields. The silence in my head put me back to sleep again. They had all disappeared and I thought I'd gotten away with not going to work. I felt so peaceful, as if death had already claimed my soul. Then I felt a jabbing pain in my chest; I'd been kicked. The Me-Krum's owl eyes penetrated my own. His army of children surrounded me, pointing their Angkar fingers in accusation. I trembled at their presence and hoped for mercy.

"Met, are you a Vietnamese spy, hidden under the blanket?" The Me-Krum whipped me with his bamboo stick. He slashed the stick across my legs to force me to get up. My body came alive again at the sound of his threats.

"Comrade, I am sick. Please, I am going to die."

"Ha, you're sick? Show me the evidence." He laughed. One of the children smacked me on the head. Another one kicked me. "Maybe this will make you feel better. Now, get to work!" I got up and started to run as if I had a stomach full of rice and chicken curry. I feared death and physical pain so much that I could will myself to run like a cowering dog to the field upon their command.

With the news that the Vietnamese were coming, we were ordered to work even harder. We dug ditches and canals, some of which became mass graves. The Khmer Rouge began to purge those they considered Vietnamese spies. Many more children died of fatigue, unable to take the humiliation, deprivation, starvation, and torture anymore. Every day I saw children and adults die and then, wrapped in blankets, get dumped in the bamboo bushes next to the temple.

The Khmer Rouge made us dig trenches and began to refer to them as "your graves." Anyone who refused an order was killed and dumped into one of the ditches. New People gossiped to one another and rumors spread in the village that the Vietnamese were indeed approaching. Most of us had never liked the Vietnamese, but I wanted them to come quickly to free me from death.

At a meeting, the Angkar Loeu said that all people, Old and New, of all ages, must be prepared to fight the Vietnamese. I thought this meeting was a trick to gather us in one place and shove us into a mass grave before the Vietnamese arrived. The Angkar Loeu told us we were his soldiers; we were nationalists defending our country. He wanted us to fight the Vietnamese to the death, to chase them away with our machetes and axes. We listened quietly, thinking secretly that sooner or later, the Khmer Rouge would be swallowed up by their own hatred and would disappear. The Angkar Loeu stood like a divine being compared to the weak and the wretched, but what had he done for us that made him think we would fight for him?

SIXTEEN

Reunion

A couple of weeks later, when the Vietnamese did attack, sometime around February of 1979, the first ones to run away in the resulting chaos were the Khmer Rouge children, who fled to their parents. I wanted them gone. Those little rats were mean and ugly. I had despised them all these years for making fun of my ears, spying on me, hitting and kicking me, and spitting in my face. When they had gone back to their nearby villages, I was free to roam the fields and look for food. I was no longer fearful of their watchful eyes. It would be a joyous day when I could finally cook my own pot of rice. My lucky teakettle had stayed with me all those dark years. It had kept me alive. My mother's spirit dwelled in it.

The temple where I was staying was almost empty. A few New kids were left. I didn't want to run just yet. I wanted to eat first. As I waited for the rice to cook, I heard a frail, female voice calling my name. I turned and saw a very gaunt young girl with sickly yellow skin.

"Do you know a boy named Seng?" she asked.

"I am Seng," I told her. "Who are you?"

"I am Theary, your sister," she replied, as if choked by tears. "Do you remember me?"

In the year since our last reunion, she had changed so much, I didn't recognize her. Her hair was uncombed and her face was like an old woman's.

"Sister? Is it you?" I said.

"Yes, it's me!" she replied.

"Oh, my God, you survived!" I began to sob amid the silence all around us.

"Where is everybody?" she asked. I couldn't stop crying long enough to tell her. We didn't know what day, month or year it was. I was too overwhelmed with joy and sadness to even describe what I'd been through or ask her how she was.

"They killed our father, and Mother died of starvation," I was finally able to tell her. I told her how they had died, how Da and Reth had died. She wept. Both of us cried so much that we lost our appetite for the rice we'd craved all those years.

Theary and I decided to look for our other brothers and sisters at the old house where Mother had died. That is where she had told us to gather in the end. Sure enough, we found our brother San sitting on the front steps, looking very tired and hopeless. We could barely recognize one another and had to introduce ourselves as children from the same womb. I had the burden of describing Mother's suffering to them. We all were so malnourished, weakened and emaciated, a storm would have swept us away like papers and leaves. San's stick like hands were touching my face, feeling it in disbelief. He looked so much like our father, well mannered and reserved. His expression was somewhere between tears and joy. He was no longer the tyrant I had known him to be when I was little.

The next day, my sister Chan came wandering by, looking like she'd lost her soul. Her head was completely shaved. Her frame was skeletal. Instead of talking to us, she talked to herself. When we told her that Mother and Father had died, she stopped talking altogether. She didn't murmur a single word. She didn't show any emotion. Those large eyes of hers looked up to pierce the sky so that it could cry for her. Between her, Theary, San, and me, the depth of our grief and suffering was left unexpressed. We couldn't even begin to put words to it. Sadness choked us up.

The Vietnamese came in green uniforms with single red stars on their helmets. They carried rocket launchers and were accompanied by tanks—it seemed as if they could conquer the world, and they had come to save us. The Khmer Rouge ran everywhere as the Vietnamese tanks rolled in from Siem Reap Province to Battambang city and razed every village on the way. This proved to be the bloodiest period of the war. The Khmer Rouge was split into two factions. One of these, the Pea Youap faction, had fled to Vietnam to avoid execution when the Khmer Rouge leaders decided to purge their ranks, killing their own people, and had returned with the Vietnamese invasion. As the two factions killed each other, I dodged their bullets and hid from the Khmer Rouge, who were disappearing into the wilderness along the Thai border. After my Me-Krum and Me-Kong were gone with the rest of the Khmer Rouge families, I came out of hiding and searched for food.

As they were abandoning Tuk Chjo, the Khmer Rouge took some of the New People with them so that we wouldn't side with the Vietnamese and attack them with our machetes, our sickles, axes, and our rage. San, Theary, Chan, and I hid in the house and waited until they were all gone. Most New People did the same thing.

Suddenly, Tuk Chjo was empty, and all the food that had been kept from us was suddenly available. Rice, cows, pigs, chickens, fruit, bamboo, and vegetables. My sisters, my brother, and I were so happy that we started to dance in a circle. Theary went to the Old People's gardens and gathered vegetables. She went into their houses and took their cooking pots and pans. I chased after chickens, but was so tired and weak that I couldn't catch one. I ended up gathering enough firewood for my sisters to cook with.

San brought back pigs, beef, and rice. Cows were slaughtered and divided among the various remaining New People. The four of us were a family again, eating our first big meal together in nearly four years. There was so much food. It was hard to eat it all. We had to take it slow at first because our stomachs weren't used to being full. I almost choked on the rice because I ate too fast.

"There's plenty of rice," Theary said. "Eat slowly, Seng." I kept shoving food into my mouth with both hands.

"You're going to kill yourself. Slow down," San said.

I ate and ate until I could hardly breathe and I could not sit down. My belly protruded like a blowfish. Theary had to take the food away, afraid that I would burst. San told me not to drink any water until my food had been digested. If I had drunk water, I would have died, which is something that actually happened to three other children. Chan ate quietly and slowly, picking at her food and chewing it in a meditative way. It seemed as if hunger had made her holy. She had been so much like my mother in her frail determination to live. Now she wasn't herself anymore. I knew there was much she had endured that I didn't know about.

We waited for things to quiet down before we started our journey back to our old home in Kampong Speu. We hoped we had a home to return to. One day, San came home with rice and chicken. He also brought the good news that it was safe to start back home.

"We're leaving in a couple of days," he said.

"Could we leave now?" I asked, eager to head home.

"Wait a few days. Many people in this village have not left yet. We'll wait and see what other people will be doing."

Now that my stomach was full, all my senses recovered. I could smell the sweet night air. My flesh regained some of its original color. I was so happy when darkness came and I didn't have to sneak out to look for food. I wished my parents were still with us. They would have liked seeing me get bigger and taller.

After most of the Khmer Rouge families left, the village was very quiet. The New People who had survived were getting ready to go home, all with the hope that home would still be there. We got our strength back after a few days. San, Theary, and Chan went to Khmer Rouge houses to collect rice, salt, and dry fish for the journey, as well as cooking utensils. I slung my mother's teakettle over my shoulder. San found a four-wheeled cart to transport water and food.

None of us knew how long it would take to walk back to Kampong Speu. During our forced march so long ago, we'd detoured and stopped in different places along the way. It had seemed like a very long distance. It would probably take us weeks. San and Theary weren't sure how to get back—we'd have to smell our way home. An exodus of people began to fill the roads once more. It was amazing to see how many people had survived. Many were alone, searching for their surviving family members.

Theary prepared another big meal and watched me closely to make sure I didn't eat too fast. Another night without hunger. I felt as if I were still in my own dream. I slept close to Theary, telling her again about how Mother, Father, and our two brothers had died. I'd told her about them two or three times after we had been reunited. That night, we slept in the house where our mother died, and I had a dream.

My parents were standing in front of the door to say good-bye to us. My mother and father were very happy. They gave me a hug and told me, "Go straight home and look after your older brother and sisters." I was the youngest and a survivor. Their spirits had kept me safe all those times.

"Why aren't you coming with me, Mother?" I asked.

"Mother can't leave this place. You go ahead, sweet boy, and we'll be very close."

"But I want to stay with you, Mother," I said.

"No, you have to go. Mother will be with you soon. Now, go. Your brother is waiting for you."

Father tried to help me put on my sackhdo (backpack), as if I were only

going off to school. I didn't want to go. It felt like something permanent. I be-
gan to cry and wouldn't let go of my mother's hand. She had to peel me away
and force me to abandon her.

Theary woke me up in the middle of the night. "Seng, Seng, what's happening?" she said, shaking me. I didn't know I had been crying.

"Mother and Father were just here. I saw them," I whispered in her ear—I was afraid I'd scare them away.

"It's OK," she said. "They're at peace now. They came to say good-bye and to let us know that they're with us. Go back to sleep. We have a long day ahead of us tomorrow."

"Is he OK?" San asked Theary, wondering why I was crying in the middle of the night. I had woken him up, too.

"He just had a bad dream," she told him.

In the morning, one of the New People told San we all should leave right away. Because if the Khmer Rouge returned, they would kill everyone they found in the village.

"Go onto the highway," he said. "It's safer. The Khmer Rouge won't come near the Vietnamese."

San panicked. He told Theary and Chan to put food and mats onto the cart. I prostrated myself in prayer for the spirits of my parents and my brothers. They were the occupants of the house now. I left them a little food and said my good-byes.

We headed out toward the main interprovincial highway, the same way we had come during the first forced march. We hoped to find our way back to the city. San's skinny hand tried to pull the four-wheeled wooden cart while my two sisters pushed from behind. Theary still had the Khmer Rouge *krama* around her neck. Her complexion was still light, but her eyes were clouded with sadness. Suddenly, we were caught up in a flood of people on this destroyed highway that was littered with bomb craters. No cars had been seen driving on it for four years. No one had been permitted on the highway. Now brothers and sisters and dads and moms— some limping with broken legs, others with blurred eyes and gaunt, frail bodies—came looking for their missing relatives. One woman came to me and asked, "Are you my son?" She kept insisting that I was her son until San pulled me away.

It was as if everyone was emerging from a grave, like zombies in search of daylight. Everyone walked slowly as if they were trying to awaken from their bad dreams.

San said we were heading toward a small bridge near the town of Krolahdown Kralanhin, Siem Reap Province. We had left Kampong Speu with a family of nine and now only four of us were making the long trek back. I dearly hoped to reunite with Yean, and wondered whether some of our brothers and sisters would be in the city when we got back. Our other older siblings Lean, Ny, and Pouv were separated from us since the Khmer took over in April 1975: we did not know what had happened to them. A few kilometers ahead, we sat under a tree, watching the Vietnamese roll onward with their tanks and munitions.

The Vietnamese smiled and waved to us with their white flags, speaking their Hanoi Communist language as our liberators. They didn't have black teeth, as we had been told, and in fact they seemed friendly and personable. Nevertheless, I didn't trust them. It could be a trick, trying to fool us just like the Khmer Rouge had done in 1975. It could mean another terror.

"We are safe now, little brother," assured Theary, and there was such happiness her face. Chan leapt back to life, smiling. San waved to his heroes. A truck full of soldiers stopped and one soldier shouted, *"Di! Di!"* which meant "Keep going." Many of us didn't understand them, but they motioned with their hands for us to keep moving forward. Then a woman emerged from the crowd and offered to be our translator. I wondered how she had hidden what she knew from the Khmer Rouge—anyone who spoke Khmer with a Vietnamese accent was killed. This woman spoke perfect Vietnamese, like my grandmother, who spoke seven different languages. She conversed freely with the soldiers and told us we had to move at least twenty to thirty kilometers away from our Khmer Rouge villages. We hoped to go even farther than that.

When we heard that the Vietnamese had taken over Phnom Penh, we decided to travel with the convoys of Vietnamese soldiers, who were proclaiming themselves our liberators. The four of us tried to get on one of those trucks. But others had the same idea. People were shoving and fighting to get on the trucks, to hitch a ride and get home fast now that the nightmare was over.

San was strong and pushed us. "Quickly! Quickly!" he shouted. "Get on now!"

Theary and Chan got on and San was trying to push me up. I tried to climb on, but I was too weak. "San, help! I can't hang on."

San came up behind me as the truck was about to move and pushed me up by the buttocks. Then he was running behind the truck. He tossed a bundle of food to us and ran to jump on.

"San, hurry! The truck is leaving," I said.

"Quick, give us your hand," Theary said. The three of us reached out and pulled him up. It was one of the happiest moments in our lives.

The truck was crowded and we could barely sit. The road was in such a poor condition that the truck jumped in the air every now and then. The breeze brushed over our smiles. Without saying a word, strangers became comrades. We understood what everyone must have been through. Secretly, however, I was worried that the Vietnamese might drop us off somewhere in the jungle. I still didn't trust them. I remembered those people who had been loaded onto a truck from Tuk Chjo village and then taken to be shot.

A few hours later, we arrived at a town in Siem Reap Province. By this time, we had run out of food. I took the open teakettle around, asking other people for rice for the rest of our journey. I had to beg, with my sad eyes and hands. A woman took pity and filled my mother's teakettle with grains of rice.

"Where is your family?" she asked.

I told her that my parents had been killed. "I now live with my three older siblings. We are going to Phnom Penh to search for more of our relatives."

The woman felt deep sympathy for my loss. She had no one left in her life. The Khmer Rouge had taken everything away from her and still she was kind to others. She followed me until we reached the shelters, where my brother and sisters were waiting. When I introduced her to Theary, she asked if I could stay with her and become her godson. Theary smiled and let out a faint laugh, but did not want to be rude to that woman. She replied respectfully but matter-of-factly, "We were a family of thirteen and only four survived. He is our youngest and we can't afford to lose him." The woman was grief-stricken. I must have reminded her of her own son.

We stayed in the city of Siem Reap for a few days to gather supplies, then continued on. The road seemed long for my small feet. I was hot and thirsty. I could not wait to finally settle down with my whole family. My brother Yean would be waiting for us, I thought. I remembered how it used to be. My mother had always prepared for holy days with sumptuous foods. Then I thought of what it would be like if my parents had lived.

San mapped the trip out to see a full picture of our travels. We would need to walk again, as the Vietnamese truck that had brought us from Siem Reap to Kampong Thom province was not going any further and we had moved on. Walking made everything seem so far away. It didn't feel as if we were making any progress. After a couple of days, we got another truck ride through Kampong Cham Province. After that, we walked. It took us almost a month to walk the final leg to Phnom Penh. Sometimes we walked in rain, sometimes in scorching sun. When we arrived, it was during the dry season of 1979. I memorized this information so that I could tell it to Yean.

We weren't out of danger yet. On the road to the capital, the Khmer Rouge made sniper attacks on us. They abducted young men into the jungle. They robbed and killed people. We were traveling in a small group and at one point our little family stopped to rest while others in the group continued on. From my resting place,

I watched the Khmer Rouge come out and kill them. They left their bodies in the fields. After that, we made sure to stay in a large crowd. The killing was not over.

Finally, we arrived at Phnom Penh, but the city gates were closed. Armed Vietnamese soldiers told us to stay out for the next few weeks. The city was still unsafe, they said. I didn't want to wait. I wanted to see the capital as it used to be, filled with people having a good time, enjoying leisure time along the riverbank, eating out, and shopping in the markets. I wanted to see the big streets and boulevards, big buildings, and the lights that should be flashing everywhere. Thousands of people were as anxious to enter the city as we were. Yet the Vietnamese said it was still dangerous.

On the outskirts of the city, we settled into an abandoned barn at a Khmer Rouge headquarters near the Pochentong International Airport, about an hour's walk from the city. Thousands of us gathered there for shelter. Some were still looking for their relatives, some were hoping that someone, anyone, would come on a plane and take them away from the wreckage. Some people found family members there, and there were many tears and shouts of joy. We settled down and waited for the city to reopen. My mother's teakettle, which had always been shiny and like new before the Khmer Rouge came, was old, rusty, and dense with stains. Theary polished it with ashes and water and we were able to use it again.

SEVENTEEN

Ghost City

The Vietnamese kept us out of the capital for days without food. We became desperate. When we heard that the Khmer Rouge had kept their food supply in the city, San and I made a plan to enter it secretly, just like old times. Several men said they would come, too. It was still dark, before three in the morning, when we left the barracks. Theary and Chan were asleep. On one of the main streets, which had been renamed Mao Tse Tung Boulevard, we heard the sound of an AK-47 firing at us. San and I leaped over a fence and ran for our lives. The other men scattered. One of the bullets flew right past my head.

"Keep your head low!" San shouted.

I ran, bending low. Between breaths, I told San how I hated that area. "Get me out of here. These Vietnamese will be after us," I said. "They might think we are Khmer Rouge or thieves and kill us." I was out of breath. San was quiet the whole time, thinking, the way my father used to do. His silence was a weapon against predators.

We waited behind some bushes until the sun came up and we could hear birds chirping among the coconut trees. Phnom Penh was empty and quiet, like a ghost town. Bombs had destroyed houses and the wreckage was everywhere. Empty villas were covered with cobwebs. Wild grasses grew in the streets. To make it worse, the Vietnamese soldiers went around collecting valuable things that the Khmer Rouge had piled up and left in the buildings. The soldiers would load them into trucks and send them to Vietnam.

San led the way, searching high and low for things to bring back to our place. Our eyes scanned the street from one end to the other on the lookout for Vietnamese. We came to a street named Kampuchea-Vietnam Boulevard. It was then that I realized that they'd kept us out because they wanted to steal valuable things and reorganize the whole city. They renamed streets to evoke the spirit of Communism and to "Vietnamize" the Cambodians. They had come to take Cambodia for themselves.

The Vietnamese had installed a puppet government led by Heng Samrin, a Cambodian, as the new head of state so that the international community could not point fingers and call their invasion of Cambodia a true takeover. The Heng Samrin government began to gather the enormous number of human remains— the axed foreheads, broken bones of hands and legs and skulls—of those who'd been murdered by the Khmer Rouge. All were dug out of mass graves and stacked away as museum pieces. They dug up the dead not only as proof of the atrocities of the Khmer Rouge but to justify their own presence. That is how we learned that the Khmer Rouge had turned Tuol Sleng High School into a torture prison.

"Look at these mass graves, these losses, the poor starved eyes of your people!" the Vietnamese said.

What if Yean is among those dug from the mass graves? I thought.

What if Yean had returned home, thinking he would become a part of the great revolution? "We need you," the Khmer Rouge had implored on international TV and radio. The young people living abroad who had returned to Cambodia when the Khmer Rouge made their promises had been taken to Tuol Sleng first and later to Choeung Ek, the killing fields, where they were executed. Or perhaps Yean had come back because he was worried about us and hadn't realized the danger he faced himself. We hoped he had remained in France. That was our dream, that he was living unharmed in France, thinking of us. I would describe everything to him and shorten the distance between us. Perhaps Yean would come back home soon and get us out of this dark place, our country, where I had suffered and no longer felt safe.

San and I came to a very imposing building on Kampuchea-Vietnam Boulevard. It turned out to be a large storage area for rice, cotton, clothing, medicine, and ammunition. We only sought rice. People just like us were there, looking for things to take, shoving rice into their bags to bring to their families. I had soon filled my bag with enough food to supply us for another two or three weeks.

Suddenly, Vietnamese surrounded us, pointing their guns at our stunned faces. I dropped the bag of rice on the ground. Everyone froze. Someone shouted a command in a language we did not understand. How could we convince them that all we wanted was food? The only word I understood was *"chet,"* or "death" in Vietnamese. If we moved, they warned, we would be dead. We raised our hands above our heads in surrender. We were taken at gunpoint to the New Olympic Stadium and held captive for several days, with hundreds of other Cambodians. They gave us some rice to cook—I found an empty turtle shell and used it as a cooking pot.

I can survive this, I thought. If I could survive all those years of torture under the Khmer Rouge, I can survive this.

After several days, the Vietnamese let us go.

When we got back to the barricades, Theary and Chan were beside themselves with worry.

"Where have you been?" Theary asked. "The Vietnamese soldiers could have killed you!"

By the time the Vietnamese opened the city, everything was gone. They were thieves, just like the Khmer Rouge, who took whatever valuables they found. The four of us decided to keep searching for our older siblings who had lived in the city and been separated from us since the arrival of Khmer Rouge. Theary tried to remember the places where they had stayed when they attended the university, and hoped that they might have returned to that place.

Yean was nowhere to be found. San had been told by some people that Yean had been killed. My only hope of getting out of this horrible place had died. I felt so empty and hopeless. My crying would not bring him back, but I let the tears flow. Father had placed so much hope in him. Yean was his brightest son.

Theary and I walked to the former prison at Tuol Sleng, where we joined hundreds of people looking for their relatives. "Come, quickly!" Theary cried. She had found Yean's name in an official prison record book. Next to it there had been a photograph that had apparently been torn out. All this suggested that Yean had been questioned at Tuol Sleng before being taken with other engineers to Chamkar Dung, the University of Agriculture. He likely was killed there and then dumped in the killing fields of Boeung Choeung Ek.

Theary and I took a horse cart out of the city to Choeung Ek. The Vietnamese had obviously not stacked all the bones and skulls of the dead. Some of the bodies were still freshly rotting. Flies buzzed around them. My heart filled with hatred for the Khmer Rouge. Yean's remains might haven been among the pile of skeletons that had accumulated between curses, slit throats, and blows of axes, their hands tied behind their backs and blindfolds on their broken skulls.

After we found out all we could about Yean, San, my sisters, and I made our way to our old house in Kampong Speu, about thirty miles outside the city. We found a house covered in vines, filled with sad memories of my brief childhood. I remembered how

I used to run here. Or how my mother had often sat on this spot. The fragrance of her cooking filled the air. Explosions had destroyed all of our rooms and bullets had left pockmarks and holes. The front entrance was covered with grass.

Theary and I reminisced about the time when we were a family, in our dining room, eating in silence. My father had never allowed us to talk with food in our mouths—it was bad manners. Everyone had to be proper and civil. He would tell us about his childhood as an orphan. "It is important to remember where you have been in order to get wherever you want to go in life," he always said.

Though our wooden and brick house was still standing, we did not want to stay. The memories of happy times were now too sad to make us want to reclaim the house for ourselves. We were afraid of the Khmer Rouge, too, because the area was still underpopulated. Phnom Penh was safer.

EIGHTEEN

Broken

The new era of government had begun rebuilding Cambodia. People were sweeping and cleaning the streets and repainting some of the buildings. Government offices were restored, and those working for the government were able to get by. The Chinese resumed business operations. Paper currency was printed again. Until then, people were trading gold for rice and meat in the market. But we had no gold. We had nothing. My mother had hidden her jewelry and the family's photographs in some bushes in Tuk Chjo, but I had forgotten about them.

So we lived unhappily in those old barracks for several months with no food or means of supporting ourselves. Our frustration and rage turned inward and kept us distant from one another. I had a lot of anger and didn't want San to control me. We fought like cats and dogs. At seventeen, San had taken on the role as head of household. He hit me if I refused to go to school, or to find food, or if I was hanging out on the streets playing cards. He wanted me to be in school and to contribute to the collecting of food. As

I saw it, education was death. What good had education done for Yean? Or Father? The Khmer Rouge had killed all the educators. With or without the gold, we all had to go out to find food. When I refused to contribute, San grew angry and threatened to strike me. I just wanted to live on the streets, a loner among other orphans. San believed we should all pull together. But I couldn't take orders anymore, from anyone.

San's eyes were rounder than mine and he appeared less Chinese than me. After all those years laboring in the sun, he had developed a darker skin tone, like the Old People. I was afraid of him because he reminded me of Rom, the Kong Chlop at the mobile camp. If my own brother could be so cruel, who else could I turn to? After what had happened to us, I had thought that we would stay together, but I was wrong. In our broken humanity, we could not distinguish our own blood relatives' intentions from the cruelty of the Khmer Rouge. The experience had made us strangers.

Eventually, we went our separate ways and left our home for new ones. Chan, who was now twenty-four, went to live with a friend, and later went to Sisophon in Battambang. San stayed in Phnom Penh and went to Orphanage Three. He wanted me to go with him, but I refused. I 'd rather scavenge and sleep on the streets. Theary, who was twenty, decided to work as a farmer in Battambang with her friends. She, too, wanted me to go with her, but I wouldn't go there. It still held nightmarish memories for me.

"You go ahead," I told her. "I think I'll try to survive as best as I can here. Don't worry about me."

"You have to come with me or else go with San to the orphanage," Theary said. "I can't leave you all by yourself."

"No, no, I don't want to live in the orphanage with him and I don't want to go with you, either."

"Where are you going to live?" she asked.

"I can survive on my own in these neighborhoods. You don't have to worry about me," I told her. That was the last time I saw Theary, Chan, and San together.

"This is all I need," I said, pointing to my bundle wrapped with a *krama*. I was the youngest in the family, so it was difficult for Theary to leave me. "I lived, didn't I?" I reassured her. Theary insisted that I go to Kolap I (Orphanage One) for children my age or a little younger. To make Theary leave, I finally agreed to go there, at least until I could roam wherever the wind would take me or the voice of my mother would tell me to go. Theary carried her little bundle, soaked with her tears, and said good-bye. "I will be in Mongkol Borei, the hut located right after a railroad bridge," she said. "Remember, if you ever need me, go there and look for me." I was relieved when she finally left. Both of us were crying. Then I was alone again, with other orphans tormenting me with their lost-looking gibbon eyes, lying to themselves that their world would get better.

NINETEEN

Princess of Phnom Penh

I spent hardly any time at the orphanage. Mostly I was out on the
streets looking for food to steal and things to see. In the dark, I felt
my way around. The streets were empty of Khmer Rouge, and the
city quickly filled with people. At Phsar Chjas, the old market, I
found people hustling for gold, trading to make the Khmer Chen
(Cambodians of Chinese descent) rich once again. Phnom Penh
came back to life, with people sweeping dirt, clearing away everything that would remind them of April 17, 1975. The bullet holes
were being repaired with new plaster and paint. The walls that
had toppled were rebuilt and new rooms were made. I wasn't sure
whether I could trust the peace even though there were people all
around me anxiously filling all the abandoned buildings. The city
seemed huge and the blue sky was too vast for my small mind. I
could roam the city all day and would never find my way around it.

I could hardly remember what it looked like before. But I re-
called clearly Phsar Thmei, the market King Sihanouk had built in
the middle of the city. My parents had taken me there often. It was

there that Yean had bought me my toy airplanes. I was surprised to see that the market was unscathed, and the central, domelike area again served as a gathering place with stalls set up everywhere. Most of the sellers were Chinese, thriving on the new economy.

At nightfall, the city was dark—there was no electricity, no running water—and all was deathly still by nine o'clock. No gatherings, no cars or motorcycles. People used horse carts. I lived on the street corners, in yards, or at the marketplace. I avoided San because I was afraid he would send me back to the orphanage.

I slept wherever I could find a spot. When daybreak came, I got up and roamed again, looking for food and work. Sometimes I helped people load goods. I was never in the same place for long. I was not alone on the street. There was always a gang of us orphans, squatting under a lamp, talking until it was time to doze off somewhere. Then the military began to patrol the streets. Whenever we saw them, we scattered like mice into the shadows.

One day a woman saw me and asked if I was Seng. I responded, "Yes! It's me." I didn't recognize her, but she told me I had played with her five children at the barracks near the airport. She asked about my siblings and shook her head in grief when I told her. Then she offered to take me into her home, saying I could work with her eldest son as a horse-cart driver. She came from a wealthy family and had been able to recover a lot of her gold, which she had buried near her home. She bought a horse and a cart for me. Soon I became familiar with most of the places in the city and every day I was able to bring home some rice.

It was back to basics in the city. Cars and buses had been replaced by oxcarts and horse carts. Our two-wheeled cart could fit five passengers at a time. As the driver, I steered the horse with a whip. People paid me in gold or rice. I gave my earnings to the woman I worked for, who in turn fed me and gave me a stipend in gold. I was all of twelve years old; in three months of working, I was able to save a few grams of gold to start my own business venture.

The woman I was living with knew how to read people's fortunes, shuffling Tarot cards and hope. I thought it was a hoax, but her incense drew people into the house. The Tarot cards were laid on the table for those who could afford it. She had a gift, perhaps, of telling people good and bad omens. I observed her, with a skeptical mind, until it was my turn to try. What lies ahead for me? I wanted to know.

"Shuffle the cards," she said. "Pick one." These were regular playing cards she was using, and a ten of diamonds came up, indicating a bright start on the road ahead. "Right now, you don't know where you are going," she stated.

I could have told you that, I thought.

"However, look here," she said, pointing to all the possibilities as she spread out the deck of cards in four rows. Her eyes lit up, as if she was going to share my good fortune. "You will have a good future when you grow up," she said. I giggled. My lips widened at the thought. "You will become an important person, more so than any of your older siblings. I see here that you will succeed in everything that you do."

I thought for a moment.

"Are you sure?" I asked.

She nodded with assurance. "In a few more years, you'll see."

I often thought about that prediction as I got up every morning at five to prepare the horse cart. I took people in and out of the market until late in the evening. As the family's gold reserve ran out, I became the rice earner for them.

One morning, the horse was gone. I panicked. I was fearful about how my patroness would react. When I told her that the horse had been stolen, she wept and sent all her children out to search for it, but it was gone. I thanked the woman for her kindness and left to go on that long journey she had seen in her cards.

Now I decided on a different survival strategy. From the gold I had saved, I would buy cigarettes and sarongs from Thailand and resell them in the capital city. It was a long way from Phnom Penh

This image representing Cambodia's golden age of music and film that took place roughly between 1960 thru 1973. It started in Phnom Penh under the rule of Prince Sihanouk who supported artistic expression of all kinds, especially film and music.

The arrival of Khmer Rouge on April 17, 1975, known as a day of betrayal in Cambodia.

(photo by Roland Neveu)

The same day thousands are forced to leave their home for the countryside, with what they can manage to carry. People were forced to work day and night in the labor camps.

This is a similar rice field at Tuk Chjor village where I worked and slept during the Years of Zero.

Interviewed by Roger Rosenblatt at the Khao-I-Dang camp in Thailand for Times magazine. I had just arrived.

(photo by Matthew Naythons)

A photograph of me at the transition camp in Thailand shortly before making my way to the U.S.

A farewell gathering for my last day at the Khoa-I-Dang camp in 1982.

First arrival in June 1982—the very first family dinner in the backyard our home in Amherst, Massachusetts. From left: Amy, Bethany, Mom, Joia, Julie, Noelle, Me and Raymond.

My second summer in the US, I'm became a normal American teenager, practiced at home before the game.

Children of War Tour group photo. Children from around the world traveled through U.S. cities in 1984 sharing their experiences of war. I am seated in the first row.

The Children of War Tours in 1984 made national news. Our-were featured in the Los Angeles Times, The New York Times and the Phil Donahue Shows. From left, me, Dessmond Tutu and Carmen Aquir.

 *In April, 1999, I returned to Tuk Chjo, village with correspondent Bob Simon from CBS's 60 Minutes— my first visit to the killing fields since 1979*

The site where I buried my mother behind the temple of Tuk Chjor village, during the same hot, dry time of year as our visit. I placed flowers and prayed.

Reunion with my three surviving siblings. From left: Theary, Seng, San and Chan in front the historical of Angkor Wat temple in Siem Reap.

My orphan friends who are now U.S. citizens and have successful carreers: 1st row from left Alyna Hillsamer, Chantha Bin, Rachel Blais: 2nd row from left Ray Bin, Narong Chum, Vuth Pich, Chuck Sart, me, Pok Dul, Sayon Soeun: 3rd row from left Thy Oeur, Hun Horn, Thy S. Horn and Chinsan Lim

My happiest day. A new chapter of my life began. November 25, 2000: our traditional Cambodian wedding in Lowell, Massachusetts.

My wonderful family, my wife Sreymom, my son Ethan and Sofia.

to Battambang and back, but I caught the train, crowded with passengers barely hanging on, and then a truck, headed for Poipet, on the border of Thailand. If it rained, I wrapped the sarongs and cigarettes in plastic and hugged them close to my body. I used the profit I made hustling goods at the central market to purchase more things. I was able to feed myself and save money to live on my own. I didn't have to beg. I saved more than five *chi* (almost two grams) of gold for an old bicycle that I hoped San could fix up someday. I was determined to work harder and take greater risks, buying products in remote areas at more favorable prices and reselling them in the city. Most people in this business were adults, but I wasn't afraid. I had taken greater risks stealing food from the fields of the Khmer Rouge.

In a few months, I had saved around fifteen *chi* of gold, which I kept in a bag that never left my side. My belly was full. I was risking my life going back and forth between Battambang and Phnom Penh. The Khmer Rouge still made sniper attacks now and then and laid down mines to blow up roads and bridges.

One day, my good fortune came to an abrupt end. I was excited because two men had come to offer me a price I could not refuse for my ten packs of cigarettes and fifteen sarongs. They were my first customers that day and if I didn't sell to them, I thought it would be bad luck. The price they offered was reasonable, so I sold them the sarongs and the gold I received was very bright. I didn't think of checking it before they left. When I finally had it tested in the market, I found it was fake. I had been tricked. I grabbed an ax from under the table to chase down the men, but they were already gone, and everyone around me thought I was crazy. I cried like a baby.

I was reduced to nothing again. Who could I turn to this time? I wondered. Soon, I was back on the street scrambling for food.

I returned to the barracks on the outskirts of Phnom Penh where we stayed when we first arrived from our long journey from

Battambang and where San and I had lived sometime near the end of 1980. I withdrew into a private world of tears and folded into myself, wanting death to be my friend. But then I started to recover and wandered out, looking for leftovers on the dusty streets. At the market, I would help people in exchange for something to eat. I lifted heavy things and in return, they would share their food. Sometimes, if I was lucky, they would give me a little gold or rice.

The new Cambodian government abolished the distinction between Old and New People. The Khmer Rouge and their children had been pushed toward the mountainous jungles in the northwest near the Thai-Cambodian border. The country came back to life again, and some families were reunited. When I saw other children playing happily in their nice tailored clothes, I saw how fortunate they were. My clothes were dirty and tattered. But I wasn't alone. Other unfortunate children wandered the streets as I did with mouths agape in search of food.

No matter what, I was determined never to go to San or Theary for help. I kept hoping that I would find my own way out of this difficult life to the future that was promised to me in the Tarot cards. The other children gazed into my blank stare and saw my dirty clothes and dirt-marked face, and they turned to pick up rocks to chase me away. They were the children of New People who had been able to reclaim the wealth they had buried and rebuild their houses. But although they were free, Angkar lurked in their cruel smiles and their renewed contempt for the poor. Some children called me names like "Garbage Boy."

Dreams of reunion sealed my eyes shut with tears every night. *"I have looked for you everywhere,"* I told my parents. *They hugged me with their smiles. Mother cooked so much food. She was feeding the neighbors, the monks, and all the children who had no parents to care for them. It was a feast. Yean came to visit when he was on vacation. My hair was combed and my clothes ironed. I ran in front of the house, flying my toy airplane. Yean looked on from a distance, and my mom watched with pride that I was her son, her future.*

I would wake up and see the city's streets leading in so many directions. Which way should I go? I heard many voices pointing the way, but I could choose only one. Then it would get to be too much, and I would curl up with a blanket over me and fight against my own screams.

TWENTY

The Train to Battambang

Early one morning I woke and looked up at the full moon and the
stars. They seemed so far away and magical. There were millions,
maybe trillions, of them, and I had only myself. I glanced over to
where I had slept and felt empty and cold. Thinking about the past
was not going to help me build a future. I thought about what the
fortune-teller had said about that long journey. I began to believe it.

For several weeks, I had thought of leaving Phnom Penh and
wondered where I would go. Like a recording, I replayed self-pity-
ing questions in my mind: Why me? What have I done in my past
life to deserve this kind of suffering?

Like a baby bird snatched by a predator, I had been peeled
away from my mother. Perhaps this was because I had separated a
mother bird and her chicks earlier in my life. I had been warned by
my mother to leave birds and insects as I found them—with their
loved ones, mother, and father, all in one family. In Buddhism, any
destruction one brings to others means an end to one's own har-
mony, and this was why all spirits fought to stay together with those

they loved. I yearned for death to end all the worries and fears in my mind. I glorified the death of others because suffering was over for them.

At that low point, I decided I was ready to leave on my long journey. I went to San at Orphanage Three and told him about my plans. I wanted him to know so that he wouldn't worry. He wasn't there, so I waited until he returned for his lunch.

"Where have you been all this time?" he said. He did not ask how I was. "Are you still at Orphanage One?"

"Yes, I am," I lied.

I knew that telling him the truth would draw a curtain between us and I was afraid he would beat me up if he knew what I was about to do. He wanted me to stay in the orphanage system and go to school.

"Here, have you eaten?" he asked, offering me some of his lunch.

"No. You go ahead and eat. I just want to tell you something."

"What?"

"I am going away," I said.

"Where are you going?"

I really didn't know. To Thailand? Or beyond? I stared at the rice on his plate. The odor from the salted beef made my mouth water.

"Somewhere far from this city," I said. Please, don't look for me. You don't have to worry about me anymore." I assured him that I could take care of myself.

"Who are you going with?" he asked.

"Alone," I said.

"You should stay at the orphanage and try to get an education," he said.

I wasn't about to let him stop me. He probably didn't think I was serious. He didn't seem confident that I could make it on my own. He thought the orphanage had been taking care of me all this time. He knew nothing about my grief or how I'd been living my own life. I hadn't seen him since he left to live in Orphanage 3.

I spent my last night on a street in Phnom Penh. Under a tamarind tree, I placed three incense sticks and a bit of rice for the spirits to keep me safe. I called on all the dead, all those in my familiar dreams, and asked them to guide me and to make sure I reached the future on the other side of the world. The ancestors were always hungry and they were always glad that I took time to share whatever I had with them. For the journey, I packed rice and dried fish, wrapped in a lotus leaf inside my *krama*. In my bundle I also folded fifty Vietnamese dong. I sat through the night, gazing at the Mekong River and picturing myself on a boat floating down upon the currents of water. I pictured my once-beloved country, Cambodia, in another boat, floating down the river with me.

The train left for Battambang right before sunrise. I knew the schedule well. I got up quietly and found my way to the station while it was still dark. I wanted to disappear on my own so that nobody would worry about me. At the main entrance people were waiting to get on the train. But I didn't have enough money for a ticket. I waited in front of the station a few minutes to see if they would be nice enough to let me on for free. I had to find a way to get on. I walked around to the side of the train station and looked left and right to see if any guards were nearby. Suddenly, the train's horn blew a warning signal. I climbed over a tall fence and jumped into the bushes. Then I saw the train start to move. I ran alongside it and asked a passenger to please give me a hand. I tossed my bundle to him and hopped on the boxcar's connector, holding onto the passenger's outstretched hand. The train was picking up speed as I dragged myself up onto the roof of the car.

On the second evening, the train arrived in Pursat. I remembered how we had passed through here on our forced march. It was raining, and I laid my *krama* under the train, hoping to sleep, but it was so painful to be back at the place that had such bad memories, I hardly slept. My feet got wet from the rain. Little frogs were jumping everywhere, playing. I prayed for the sun to come up so that I could leave. A couple of hours before sunrise, I fell asleep.

Then I heard the loud whistle of the train. It was time to go. The crowd began to claim their spots on the train.

Oh, Buddha, I thought, getting up shakily. I grabbed my bundle and got out from under the train as quickly as I could.

Late afternoon on the third day, my train arrived at Battambang City, the transfer point for the import-export traffic between Cambodia and Thailand. Most of the other passengers had come from Phnom Penh to see their homes or relatives. I didn't have any family or friends with whom I could stay. So I stayed in the central market after the people had gone home. It was a great spot. Many other homeless children were hanging out there. I decided I would call it my home, too. No one seemed to bother us, and I figured that if other children could survive, I could, too.

The next morning, at the marketplace, I heard a man calling, "Mongkol Borei and Sisophon! Mongkol Borei and Sisophon!" I didn't have enough money to get on the truck. I held onto a woman's bag and pretended I was her son so they wouldn't charge me. At noon on the same day, I arrived at Mongkol Borei and went to search for Theary. I found her living in a small hut with friends. She hugged me.

"What are you doing here?" she asked.

"I'm here to say good-bye," I said.

"Where are you going?" Theary asked.

"Somewhere far away," I said.

Theary didn't believe me. She gave me some leftover food, which I ate gratefully. Her daily living was a struggle, but she asked me to stay with her. "You are too young to go alone," she said. "You should stay in one place and start going to school." But I was determined. My mind was already made up to leave this country and I knew that my mother's spirit would guide me. That night, Theary told me of her struggle and how she was surviving day by day in Mongkol Borei. She didn't have much food. We lit a lamp in the little hut and I looked at her skinny face and saw how sad she was.

"Sister, do you want to come with me?" I asked.

She smiled and apparently thought I was joking. She was very concerned about my life. She felt like she was responsible for looking after me.

In the early morning, I made rice soup for breakfast and prepared to leave. Theary couldn't stop me. She cried and begged me to stay. She would take care of me, she said. She didn't want to lose another one of the family. She couldn't believe I was actually leaving her. I was waiting for an oxcart to come by. I told Theary not to worry about me.

"If you don't see me coming back in ten days, I will be somewhere far away. If I die, I will visit you in a dream. I know how to take care of myself."

Tears fell from her eyes and she carefully listened to me. "I am not a little boy," I continued. "I can survive on my own, so Sister doesn't need to worry about me."

Theary was kind. She pulled out some Thai baht from her side pocket and paid for the oxcart driver. I thanked her for her generosity.

"You take care, I will miss you," I said.

As the cart was taking off, I yelled to her that I would come back someday. And I waved back to her. She was standing there until we could no longer see each other.

Sisophon was my last stop, for I needed to say good-bye to Chan. I found her there and told her everything, but she couldn't prevent me from leaving either. She packed some food and water for me to take. "Sister, I give you my word, I am old enough to take care of myself," I assured her. Both of my sisters worried that I would be forced to join the soldiers in the jungle.

TWENTY ONE

The Predators

The next morning I walked to the station in the center of Sisophon, where oxcarts were waiting to take customers. I saw one cart full of people headed for the village of Nymit, just over the border from Thailand. I snuck behind and hopped onto the cart along with ten or fifteen other passengers. I asked a woman for a little spot to sit in and she squished in to provide a tiny place for me. The cart was heading to Nymit, where the people would buy Thai products to sell in the cities. Some people paid to be taken across the border, although most people who bought and sold Thai products knew how to get around and easily crossed it. I had no money except my fifty Vietnamese dong from the city. In this part of the country people used Thai baht. The owner of the cart went around to collect Thai baht, but he didn't collect from me—he must have thought I was that woman's son. I was very nervous as we headed northwest to the Thai-Cambodian border. It was midday, and the sun was hot when we came to a checkpoint. Oh, Buddha! I thought. The military guards told us to go inside the hut. One of the guards, his

AK-47 rifle on his shoulder, approached me and asked, "Where are you going?" I paused a second, thinking how I should answer him. Then he yelled, "Are you escaping Cambodia?"

"No, no, *bong*," I said. *Bong* means brother. "I have no intention of leaving Cambodia." In a shaky voice I said, "I heard people go to the border to get rice."

He didn't believe me. He brought me to the back of the hut. I said to myself, Oh, Buddha, is he going to shoot me or has he just tricked me? I told him I'm not Vietnamese. Why would they think I am a Vietnamese boy? I speak the same Khmer language. There are a lot of Vietnamese families escaping through Cambodia to Thailand—maybe they think I'm one of them.

The minute I heard him say "Bring him to the prison camp," I started crying and begged him to please let me go. Suddenly, he asked if I had any cigarettes. I knew that he wanted something from me. I took my fifty dong and gave it to him. He let me go with the rest of the people.

At about six o'clock in the evening, I arrived at Nymit's central market, where most of the produce arrived from Thailand. While I wandered around looking for some rice to eat, I heard some refugees gossiping about a group leaving for the Nong Chan Refugee Camp that night. At sunset, a group of people gathered, some with bikes, some with bags, ready to cross the border into Thailand. One man went around the group collecting gold to pay for a guide through the jungle.

The sky was cloudy and the air was humid. I followed the group heading to the forest. "What is this little boy doing here?" a man said. Men and women in the group said, "Go home, you're too little to come with us." I kept following. It was so dark and quiet, I heard only crickets everywhere in the jungle. In my head, I was worried about Vietnamese and Khmer Rouge soldiers. On the ground, I was so scared of stepping on land mines and wild animals. Far in front of me, the group moved deeper into the jungle and I tried to keep up with them. I didn't feel tired because my thoughts were of life and death. I walked miles and miles through this jungle.

At midnight, I was following the group along a small trail in the middle of nowhere. I tried to keep my eyes and ears alert and stay close to the group. I was scared and very nervous of losing them. It was a long night. Suddenly, we came to the Khmer Rouge checkpoint. We were surrounded. The man who led the group told everyone not to run.

"It's our comrades," I heard a man's voice telling us.

I will die in this jungle! I thought.

It was dark, but I could see that they wore black uniforms. I stood in the group, waiting for what was going to happen next. My body was a little shaky from seeing the machine guns on their shoulders. The man who led the group walked off to negotiate with the soldiers. After a few minutes he came back and said we must give the comrades cigarettes or Thai baht to cross the checkpoint. A voice asked the group to search for any Vietnamese spies within the group. Oh, no! I was terrified the group might turn me in to the soldiers. I grabbed a handful of dirt and scrubbed my shiny skin to make it little darker. I was sweating and thinking I would die at the hands of the Khmer Rouge after all. I called on my mother to save my life. I told her I was in trouble and I didn't want to die alone in this jungle. *"Please help me to get though this, Mother,"* I prayed.

After about a half hour, the Khmer Rouge soldiers asked for the Thai baht. I panicked because I didn't have any. Everyone gave the Khmer Rouge money or gold to get past the checkpoint. Slyly, I walked close behind one of the women, pretending to be her son. As she paid the bribe, I stood behind her. I crossed the checkpoint stealthily and the Khmer Rouge didn't notice me. Well beyond the checkpoint, I prayed again to my mother's spirit and thanked her for being there to save my life. I knew she was watching her little boy venturing off to find his new life.

I had told myself that whatever happened to me in this jungle, I would never give up and return to Cambodia. I would feel ashamed if I had to go back to the city and see my brother and sisters. I needed to keep my positive dream alive. If I die in the jungle, I thought, I will be reunited with the dead members of my family somewhere in heaven. That is why I was so brave and put all the fear behind me and walked with the group on the trail of darkness to meet the dreams I had.

Thai thieves were waiting along the way. We heard a gunshot and then several more. Everyone scattered into the bushes. Elephant grass slashed through my shirt and sharp thorns scraped against my bare feet. My body was soaked with dew. I felt itchy all over. The Thais told everyone to come out. They said they wouldn't hurt us if we did. Some people believed them and gave themselves up. I stayed put. Two older men were hiding near me. One man told the other that we were somewhere close to the Nong Chan camp. It was only a couple of kilometers away. I didn't know these two men, but I tried to keep close to them. They didn't want me to follow them because I was too small to keep up. I would be a burden to them. I tried not to fall asleep, but my body was too exhausted from running. The next thing I knew, the men were gone. They could have woken me up, but they decided to leave me there. I had lost my bundle of food and clothes while running from the thieves. I was wearing only shorts and a torn T-shirt. The Thais were shining their flashlights looking for us.

I must have wandered for days in the jungle, taking my chances. The sun sent its heat to my pale white skin and pointed me west. Freedom was somewhere in the direction of the setting sun. Again, I cried out to my mother to guide the way. I was sure that the next time I got caught I would surely die. I was also afraid of stepping on land mines. I never thought I would be scared of happy-sounding birds, but I was. The trees stood so tall. There could be wild animals, like tigers, in the wild grass, which stood taller than I did. I had never felt so unsafe. My only comfort was thinking of my mother and praying that she would point me toward the refugee camp. My teeth were chattering from cold every night.

I found a small trail and followed it westward for a distance. To distract myself from thinking about death, I talked to myself. As I was walking along this trail, I heard a gunshot. A bullet flew close to my face, missing me by several inches. I dove to the ground, shaking like a mouse. I'm dead, I thought. This time I'm going to be dead. I always thought of worst-case scenarios whenever I felt I was in danger. I started to cry.

"Who is crying?" asked a Khmer voice. I didn't move.

"Come on out. Put your hands over your head or we are going to shoot."

I stood up with tears in my eyes, begging, "Please do not shoot. I'm lost."

I was so relieved to see Para soldiers! I could tell by their uniforms. The Para soldiers had been freedom fighters, recruited and trained by Thailand, and still loyal to King Sihanouk. I didn't realize that they still existed.

"What are you doing over here all by yourself?" one of them asked. It was comforting to know they cared.

"I came from Phnom Penh," I said.

"Who did you come with?"

"I followed a group of people last night from Nymit, but we were separated after Thai thieves chased us."

"Do you realize how dangerous this place is?" one of the soldiers said. "You're too little to be in a place like this by yourself." He was tall, with a uniform that looked like one that a Lon Nol soldier would have worn. He was kind. I told them I was looking for my relatives and didn't want to go back to Cambodia. I was afraid they would send me back.

"Please, take me to Nong Chan Refugee Camp," I asked.

TWENTY TWO

Caged with Barbed Wires

I was glad when the barbed-wired gate opened for me to enter. The refugee camp was another prison, perhaps, but it was safer than the jungle and definitely better than Cambodia. I walked down a red dirt road into the camp, checking out my new environment. Blue tents and bamboo huts were lined up in rows that seemed to stretch for miles. I was so thirsty all of a sudden. I approached a woman who was giving her baby son a bath and asked, "Ming"— Ming means Auntie—"may I have some water to drink?" She gave me some.

Ahead, I saw a large crowd gathered in what turned out to be a lively marketplace. It felt like home in Kampong Speu. The smell of food made me hungry, but I didn't have money. I saw a woman feeding her son and daughter noodle soup. I wanted some soup, but I couldn't go to her and ask for it. Like an obedient dog, I waited for the kids to finish eating, then grabbed the plates and gulped down whatever was left. The woman saw me licking the plates and started to shout, "Go away! Shoo! This is not a temple. It's a marketplace.

You go away. Shoo! Go, now!" Then she said, "Your parents don't feed you?"

I dropped the plate on her table and ran, my stomach filled for another day. I continued to roam the market, thinking of ways to survive there. I didn't come up with any schemes but was happy relaxing in the sun. My body was so sore. I remember sitting under a tree for a while, trying to think of a plan. Night approached and people started to return to their huts and tents. I was still hoping to run into somebody I knew who would take me in. When I didn't find anyone, I went back to the empty market and cried.

I had no clothes to change into, no blanket, and no food. I slept that night under a tree, on a torn mat I had found by one of the market stalls. There was a full moon above and tears flooded down my cheeks. I yearned for my mother. I missed my brother and sisters. A woman walked by and told me to go home because it was dark.

"I have no place to stay," I told her. "I escaped from Phnom Penh and I just got here this morning." I guessed she didn't like city people that much. She reacted as if she wanted to spit at me. People from Phnom Penh must have done something bad to her.

"Where is your family?" she asked.

"I am an orphan. I'm here alone," I told her.

"Fine," she said. "You can stay with me tonight and in the morning I'll take you to register with the Red Cross." She turned out to be very kind. She took me to her hut, gave me a *krama* as a washcloth and towel, then a plate of rice and tuna. I didn't leave a single grain of rice on the plate.

In the morning, she took me to the bamboo office of the International Rescue Committee (IRC) and told me to wait until the workers arrived. I thanked her by clasping my hands and bowing. After a couple of hours, a Toyota truck pulled up in front of the office. Three Westerners and a Thai man got out of the truck. There was a line of people waiting to be registered so that they could stay in the camp and receive food and water. I was the third in line. I told the Thai man who interviewed me that I had escaped from Cambodia alone and my parents and all of my relatives had been killed by the Khmer Rouge. He said I would have to go to an orphanage at another camp in Thailand called Khao-I-Dang. Nong Chan Camp didn't have an orphanage. He told me to stay there and wait for him. Through the translator, he said he would do whatever he could to get the paperwork processed in Bangkok and take me to Khao-I-Dang Camp in a few days. Meanwhile, he placed me temporarily with a Cambodian family he knew.

For a week, I waited at the family's tent with great hope and anticipation of going to Khao-I-Dang. The man was very kind. Every day, when he came to work he brought me cookies and new clothes. One day I was told to wait in front of the IRC office to be taken to Khao-I-Dang. A small army jeep came with two other foreign workers and a Thai driver to take me away. I was the only one to go.

I arrived at Khao-I-Dang on Friday, August 7, 1981. I remember going through a Thai checkpoint near Aranyaprathet. I remember thinking that I was no longer at the border, but safe inside Thailand. Thai guards came up to the driver and started to question him. One of the foreigners got out of the jeep and walked toward the little guard post. Khao-I-Dang was a strict camp, and no one could go in or out without permission. Finally, the gate opened. I felt like a prince entering his palace grounds. But as soon as I scanned my surroundings, I saw it wasn't really a palace. I was actually a prisoner.

If I were a prince, there had been a revolution. I had been overthrown and taken away from my city of pagodas and palaces.

Two rows of barbed-wired fences surrounded the camp, which was at the foot of a mountain. A clay road zigzagged through barren land. Outside, and in their guard towers, Thai soldiers were on constant lookout. They patrolled the area with M16 automatic rifles, keeping us in and others out. Yet refugees kept coming. Some managed to cut the barbed wires and sneak in. I was lucky I had been brought there legally—I didn't have to worry about being shot. The camp was very crowded, with clusters of straw huts. But trucks delivered rice and water, and there were boxes of meat and vegetables handed out, and that felt like heaven. The Cambodian people lined up for their daily aid packages. People in charge of the Orphanage Center, Section 23AB, greeted me and handed me over to a new Pa and Mak, (more like babysitters than real foster parents) who gave me a towel, mat, spoon, blue plastic bowl, cup, pair of sandals, toothbrush, toothpaste, blanket, and mosquito net, and then led me to a bamboo dormitory shared by twelve other children. They welcomed me with curiosity.

I was taken to the kitchen and given a big bowl of rice and salted fish. Every time I had food, I felt so grateful. I devoured every bit and licked the bowl clean. I finally felt I would never go hungry again. There were people here who would not abandon me. I was safe again. That evening, I had my first dessert in years: rice pudding and sweet potatoes encrusted with coconut and sugar. After I had the sweets, I came alive. Every part of my body wanted to run and scream for joy. For almost four years I had craved it. I slept through the night still tasting the sweetness on my tongue. Something right was finally happening for me.

Thailand may have been peaceful, but it was still very poor. It was obvious that the Thai soldiers wanted to be somewhere else earning a better wage. If they couldn't, they'd be satisfied keeping us locked up and making what money they could from humanitarian organizations. One day we would all be resettled—it was just a matter of time, and the Thai guards knew it. Consequently, they abused us as much as they could to let us know they were superior. They would come into the camp after the foreign workers left for the day.

Like the Vietnamese, the Thai had been the enemies of the Cambodians. They were the tigers who wanted to swallow us up one side, while the Vietnamese were the crocodiles who bit us from the other. In addition, the Thai feared the Vietnamese and used the Cambodians as a buffer.

The Mak who looked after the orphans warned me not to go anywhere near the barbed-wire fences. Thai guards would shoot anybody trying to get out or in.

My orphanage was at the far end of the camp at first and then, a few months later, I was moved from section 23A to 23B, two blocks from the fence. It was near the girls, and I could hear their screams when Thai guards would abduct them and rape them at night.

Even the Khmer Rouge had not raped or tortured girls like the Thai guards did. They were criminals and murderers in positions of power. They left those girls with permanent scars in their hearts and minds.

More than ten of us boys were squeezed onto a single bamboo bed in 23B. The boys were already my friends and brothers, and now that we lived so closely, the girls became my sisters, too. I remember one night when our screams chased away a drunken guard looking for a girl. Most humanitarian workers left at the end of the day, so they didn't know what was really going on at night, when the guards would get drunk and rape the girls. Parents would sleep on both sides of their daughters to protect them, but the orphaned girls had only each other.

TWENTY THREE

Waiting and Hoping

Life in Khao-I-Dang was going well for me. Truckloads of food were brought in by humanitarian organizations such as the United Nations High Commissioner for Refugees (UNHCR). I received three meals a day. It was a treat to have a full bowl of rice, tuna fish, and fresh fruit—grapes and papaya to sweeten our teeth. I had forgotten how these things tasted and relished them with slow bites. The grapes were especially juicy. The rest of life in the refugee camp was about waiting. For a while, we felt undeserving of all the handouts we were receiving, but that didn't stop us from waiting for the trucks every day. I had lost interest in school—I couldn't absorb what I was supposed to learn. This is what San didn't understand when he used to lecture me about the importance of education. My mind was far away from the refugee camp. I had heard that America would guarantee my freedom and security, and so English was the only thing I was interested in learning.

A man in a Toyota came asking for me one morning. "I am looking for a boy named Ty Kim Seng. Is he here?" he asked Pa.

"He's the boy who arrived recently from the border," Pa said, pointing to me.

The man introduced himself as Yuom, a Cambodian translator in the office of the IRC. "You have an interview with the International Rescue Committee," he said.

"Interview? Will I get to go to another country?" I asked.

"No," he said. "They just want to talk to you."

At the IRC office, a white man got up from his bamboo chair and greeted us. He was tall, with blue eyes and curly hair. I came up only to his thigh. I was afraid to look up at him.

"My name is Neil Boothby," he said, pointing to himself. His eyes glistened and his smile was warm. He wanted to know where I had been and how I had fled so far all by myself. Yuom, who was translating, said the American was a child psychologist from Harvard University in Cambridge, Massachusetts, and wanted to ask me a few questions. I didn't know what a psychologist was or where Massachusetts was, but I understood he had come to interview me about my life's experience.

This was the first of many interviews with Neil Boothby. I didn't tell him that I had a brother and sisters still living in Cambodia because I feared he would send me back or prevent me from immigrating elsewhere. Before he left, he assured me that one day I would be resettled in America. And he brought me a new set of clothes.

One day, I was trying to solve mathematics problems on the blackboard when Yuom came looking for me. He told my teacher to dismiss me. Everyone thought I was leaving for America as we drove away.

"There are two American journalists here to interview you," he said. "Maybe you will soon be able to leave this crazy camp."

I was very nervous and excited. One man introduced himself as Roger Rosenblatt and the other, holding a camera, as Matthew Naythons, from *Time* magazine. While Roger Rosenblatt interviewed me, with Yuom translating, Matthew Naythons took pictures of me at different angles. Mr. Rosenblatt gave me some crayons and a few sheets of paper. "Draw," he said. "Draw anything." Yuom explained that I was to draw whatever came to my mind.

I thought for a while before I began. I wanted to draw what I'd gone through, but couldn't put it all on one sheet of paper. So I drew my skinny body standing under a tree, a reference to the time I was starving at the mobile team work site. Then I drew myself nearly dead from malnutrition and overwork, and standing under a tree trying to eat leaves. But I also wanted to draw something happy. I imagined an airplane and drew one, remembering my airplane toys and the flights with my mother to her hometown, and the long wait for Yean to come home from France for visits, and my dream of becoming a pilot, so that is what I drew—an airplane that would take me to America.

Then Roger Rosenblatt and the photographer left. A few weeks later, Yuom was also leaving. It seemed as if everyone was leaving me. Yuom had become familiar to me and whenever he came for me, I felt happy. One afternoon, several buses came for him and other refugees.

"Don't worry," he said, "you're going very soon."

It was easy for him to say. I couldn't wait to get out. I had been there for almost eight months by then, in constant fear of the Thai guards. For months, I watched the friends I'd made leave. Some went to France. Others to America or Australia. Buses came for them and they would disappear to safety and freedom. I felt abandoned. Every night, I burned incense in the hope I would be taken to a great country where children didn't have to go hungry.

Sometimes at night, the orphans who remained would sit in a circle of candlelight, fantasizing about America. Thul, the oldest, was the best storyteller. Sometimes Thul would tell us ghost stories that made every one of us afraid, or kung fu stories or adventures or cowboy stories. It was like watching a movie. We didn't have electricity, radio, or television. We had to stay in our huts when darkness fell. We would huddle together to listen to his ghost stories. He kept us scared and hopeful. One night, Thul told us about a boy who fell from an airplane through the bathroom's toilet. Nobody knew that the boy had fallen until the plane landed and his parents discovered he was missing. Thul warned us not to touch anything, especially in the bathroom, if we ever got on an airplane.

Among the orphans, I knew Sinoun, Narin, Ny, Rim, Phon, Chey, Horng, and Thorn best. They followed me because I was the most aggressive, bravest, and most outspoken, even though I had been the last to arrive. They were all fourteen or fifteen years old. I was thirteen. We all had chores and took turns sweeping the ground, weeding and watering the garden, and bringing water from the well to the kitchen.

One day, I learned that there was going to be an adult soccer game in the camp and convinced them to skip school and go to the game. I had never seen a soccer game in my life and didn't want to miss it. "We have to go," I said. "Our Cambodian team is playing against the Thai from Bangkok."

"What if Pa finds out?" worried Sinoun.

"Don't worry! He's not going to find out," I said.

But Sinoun didn't want to be caught. "If Pa finds out, he will beat us for sure," he said.

"Look, I'm going with or without you," I said.

"Ok, I guess I'll go, too," he said finally.

As I was small, I tried to get into the front row so I could see close up. It was exciting to cheer on as the Khmer team scored a goal. In the end the Thai would win, however. It was a set up that the Khmer team would let them to win so that the Thai guards wouldn't in a bad mood and come into the camp beating people without reason.

We snuck back before dinner and Father Pa didn't say anything, but around noon the next day he called us.

"Who skipped school yesterday?" he asked. Everyone was quiet.

"Kneel," he ordered. Everyone got whipped because they refused to tell him that I had been the ringleader. But their eyes were pointing at me and he could sense I was the culprit. I received the worst beating. It didn't hurt because I had already been beaten so many times by the Khmer Rouge. Then Pa demanded that we kneel for a long time on the rocky ground. It was very hot but we weren't allowed to complain or cry.

Thorn, my closest friend, was thin and fragile but the friendliest person I knew. He was gentle and soft-spoken like Sisovatha, the royal prince in my mobile camp, and always good to other people. I began to pal around with him and he encouraged me to take English lessons with him. He always carried his *Essential English* book; he made learning the language the center of his life. It allowed him to dream of a future.

"If we are going to go to America, we have to study English," he said.

We decided to save some fruit and exchange it for Thai baht to pay for English classes. We thought, they're our ticket out of the camp to America. One day, when Thorn returned from his English lesson, all the good fruit had been taken and he accused me of leaving him only rotten fruit. He thought I had taken the good fruit to sell.

"I don't know what happened," I told him. He pushed me and the next thing I knew, we were punching each other. My nose was bleeding and his eyes were black and blue. The other orphans were watching as we fell on the ground and began pulling each other's hair. We didn't talk to each other for weeks. Then one morning, out of the blue, he ran after me, calling out my name.

"Seng! Seng!" he said. "I have good news for you. People from the IRC were looking for you."

"Who?" I asked.

"A woman came a few minutes ago and told me your name is posted at the IRC's office for America," Thorn said.

"My name? Are you sure?"

"You're going to America!" he shouted.

I ran out of the school and jumped up and down. Everyone in my classroom thought I was going out of my mind. But it was true; My name was there, among hundreds of other orphans, on the list to be resettled and adopted. Thorn and I became friends again. I said good-bye to him three days before my departure. Finally, I was free from the cage. I had been in Khao-I-Dang for eight months.

In Cambodia, people capture little prairie birds, cage them, and sell them during special holidays. Those who buy them can release them for religious merit. But birds should not be caged. They are meant to be free. I was meant to be free. Theary, Chan, and San were still in their cages somewhere in Cambodia. I could smell America from a distance. Freedom was only a few days away.

TWENTY FOUR

On Another Continent, Someone Was Thinking of Me

One morning, a woman went to the mailbox to retrieve her mail. It was one of those icy-cold New England mornings, and she had to scurry back into the house. She glanced at the issue of *Time* magazine, which she received on a regular basis. On the front page, the title "Children of War" grabbed her attention. In the house, warm and cozy, she settled down with a cup of tea. *Time* was the first thing she picked up, and she flipped through its pages. In it were stories of children who had lived their entire lives in war-plagued countries. Photographs of young children with sad eyes sought her attention. Sure enough, I caught it. She had read and heard of Cambodian orphans in refugee camps through the humanitarian work of New England clergyman Reverend Peter Pond prior to her interest in these stories written for *Time* by Roger Rosenblatt.

Rosenblatt interviewed many war-affected children to test his theory that children, in spite of all these horrible things they witnessed, may possess certain qualities of compassion and forgiveness. Is it possible to forgive? He asked.

I was one of the children he interviewed. He wanted to know whether I believed in revenge. Since I had lost most of my family members to the genocide carried out by the Khmer Rouge, Rosenblatt wanted to talk to me. And that interview was what eventually connected this woman to me. The rest was a miracle, a chance so far beyond what I could ever have imagined.

"Do you believe in revenge?" Mr. Rosenblatt had asked. His cameraman clicked a picture. My eyes black, my face full of hope, a child wanting a new home. I called out for someone out there in America to take me soon, hoping to get out of that place, that refugee camp full of violence and hopelessness.

"Yes," I told him, not understanding what it meant. The woman read on. I wasn't done explaining.

"Do you want to kill those who killed your parents and your siblings?"

"No," I told him. "I don't want to kill anybody. My only revenge is to be the best person possible, and to be as good a man as I can be."

The woman thought that was wise. Tears flowed down her face as she finished the article. She didn't know what to do. She wanted to carry the wisdom of my message and share it with others. Yet, it wasn't enough. She wanted to *be* my voice. She could even be my arms and legs, walking, reaching out as extensions of her own self, her humanity. She had the power that I did not have, the power of peace, the power of wealth and freedom. All she needed now was my words. The power of revenge isn't in the act of killing, but in the act of goodness. With this realization, this woman spent the next six months sharing my words with others throughout Southern New England, encouraging them to take an orphan into their home. Inspired by the work of Rev. Pond, and by what I said, she made the plight of Cambodian orphans her business and her mission, urging friends and strangers to give a future to so many children in destitution hoping for a new home, a bed to sleep in, and a school to go. Her name was Marlena Brown.

Through her talk and hard work, Lutheran Social Services heard her and opened its doors to help settle unaccompanied Cambodian minors in Western Massachusetts through an individual family adoption program. A similar program was already taking place in Boston. The woman was offered a job as the director of that program. Encouraged by the hope that there would be enough children leaving the refugee camps, she accepted.

Before she was offered this work, she had taught at school on a volunteer basis, but this was a chance to do what she loved and get paid. She also wanted to make sure that she could still adopt a child, and when the answer was yes, she prepared for her new job and the arrival of her new son. She said she specified a boy because her eldest child wanted to have a brother after having lived with five younger sisters.

Finally, they started seeing progress made in moving Cambodian orphans out of the refugee camps and into American homes. The Lutheran Social Service Program was finally able to receive children. The woman received a call from Reverend Bill, her supervisor from the main LSS office in Framingham, Massachusetts, telling her that the first two boys were being released and would arrive in two weeks. He asked her whether she wanted to adopt one of them. One would think that having waited so long for this moment, she would have answered with a resounding yes, but the timing was not good. Her second-eldest daughter was graduating from Amherst Regional High School, and she did not want to take attention away from her daughter's achievement. She also felt that the child coming to them after such a long ordeal had waited for so long that he should have the family's full attention. Her family agreed. "Let other orphans settle first before we adopt," they advised.

A month later, two more boys were released from the refugee camp. This time the woman and her family were ready. Another call from Reverend Bill said he would be sending the files on the boys and that he had arbitrarily assigned one of the boys to her. However, if for any reason she wanted to change the assignment, she should feel free to do so. The two files arrived just in time for the journey from Amherst to the airport near Hartford, Connecticut. The boys' names were penciled on the files, along with the name of the family to which each was assigned. She noticed that both boys had "Kim" in their name. As she held the files, something deep within her whispered for her to erase her name from the one "Kim" file and put it on the other "Kim" file. A sudden calmness settled in her heart as she changed the names, and she knew she was now ready, and the "rightness" of her action settled into her being.

All six of her own children were with her at the airport, even those who had already left home, gone to college, and now were living their own independent lives. She believed they all sensed something important was about to happen. The plane finally landed, and the family strained to see their son and brother among the weary travelers who streamed off the plane.

Finally, two boys could be seen wearing the distinctive parkas given by the refugee resettlement agencies to keep the refugees warm as they came into the colder climes of New England. But their thong sandals were reminders of the old lives they had left behind in the warmth of Southeast Asia. One boy was much smaller than the other, and had a look of confidence the other did not have. The woman seemed to be in a daze as she felt someone pull her sleeve to awaken her. "That's him! That's him!" the voices shouted. "The boy from the magazine." As the boy approached, she knew. She knew from the large brown almond-shaped eyes, and the ears that seemed a bit too large for his face, that it was me, the boy who had inspired her with his unusual concept of revenge. The woman's heart soared. She never thought she would have me as part of her household, but it was a real miracle that this happened.

TWENTY FIVE

Like a Bird with Wings

After being released from Khao-I-Dang, I was sent to Chunburi
Camp in Thailand and confined, once again, until all my documents were finalized. It took two months. Every morning I visited the bulletin board where the names of those accepted into
the United States were posted. One morning, I saw my name—
an American family had adopted me! Strangers from afar would
soon be waiting to welcome me into their home. I checked and
rechecked to make sure I was really the lucky one.

"I am going to America!" I shouted. All my friends were very
happy for me, but they, too, wanted to leave. Their faces of sorrow
and pain shrouded my sunshine.

One day, a very large man from the US Immigration and
Naturalization Service interviewed me with a young interpreter
half his size. One look at him and every nerve in my body shook.
He had a huge gold chain around his neck, and the tattoos all over
his arms made me tremble. He was the official whose job it was to
interview everyone coming to the United States. Maybe America

wasn't the dreamland I had imagined, if he was the one making decisions about which refugees would be allowed to resettle in America and which ones wouldn't. Many Cambodians painted him as evil because he wouldn't let them pass his interview easily. He looked like a soldier. His hair was cut short. His eyes were sky blue like a Siamese cat. One question asked, one answer given.

Finally, he said I should raise my right hand and swear some kind of an oath, the final step to going to America. I had passed! Was it luck? Who had chosen me? Many people were waiting to be where I was standing.

I couldn't help but think of all the people who had never made it this far. Da's faint, swollen call sounded loudly in my heart. He had sent me on this journey to live for him. My father would be very proud because his name would survive through me. I would live to tell the tale of hardship and pain. My mother's faint screams pricked me with sadness.

A few weeks before I was to leave, a letter arrived. No one had ever written me a letter! Inside was a twenty-dollar bill with a brief note I could neither read nor understand. But I recognized the name: Neil Boothby. I wondered how he knew I was going to America. Twenty dollars turned into hundreds of Thai baht, with which I purchased clothes and shoes for myself and for other orphans.

From Chunburi, they shoved those of us going to America into a bus and took us to Lumpeni, a crowded, prison like camp in Bangkok where refugees were quarantined before leaving the country. I could hear the bustling city noises of Bangkok and smell the rotten sewage and vegetables. I heard cars, buses, trucks, and motorcycles from dawn till dusk. I peeked through the gate to glimpse what was outside.

I imagined America would be even bigger and busier than Bangkok was. I had seen photos and posters showing America was like a Hollywood movie dreamland, with green rolling hills and wide-open spaces. There was no violence or suffering there. Outside the window of my imaginary American home, I saw peace and heard birds. Children ran and played on freedom's ground. A plane would take me there, the same way Yean had left for France.

I waited impatiently for two more days. Will the family like me? I wondered. Will I have brothers and sisters? The INS didn't give me any information about the people who were adopting me. Had the people who wanted to adopt me seen my picture in Roger Rosenblatt's *Time* article? My mind buzzed with high hopes for my family and myself. I didn't care about the noisy mosquitoes or the smell of raw sewage next to the barn where I was sleeping.

At last, June 16, 1982 arrived, the most joyous day of my life. "Good-bye, camp," I whispered. "I am going to a new place, but nothing will make me forget what I have experienced."

On the way to the airport, I tried to take in everything. Bangkok was a beautiful modern madness. There were throngs of people walking and driving. It was a paradise compared to Cambodia. I flashed back to being in a car in Phnom Penh before the Khmer Rouge came. In another flashback I was walking along the street with my parents and Yean. Bangkok was never as grand and beautiful as Phnom Penh was in those days. Nothing matched the beauty of Cambodia then, but it was now reduced to a pile of trash and destroyed lives. I was moving forward, though. I would soon be going to school and acquiring the strength to avenge my mother's death with knowledge. Her soul would not rest in peace until she knew I was all right. I felt her presence every step of the way.

At Bangkok International Airport, a group of orphans including my friend Kim huddled together in an isolated building for hours, forging a close bond, We each shared a dream, a story, or a few thoughts about what we imagined America would be like. We didn't know what was in store for us, and we had a good laugh as we talked about ways we could cope with the new world. We watched the airplanes taking off and landing. Soon we, too, would be free.

The smaller children screamed—they were sick, traveled-out, and hungry. It was already close to midnight. "Have you been on a plane before?" one of the orphans asked. His name was Kim.

"I saw my brother go on a plane once," I said. "And I was in a small plane flying to my mother's hometown. But not a big one. It's so big, I wonder how it can get off the ground and fly across the ocean." None of us knew the answer. The jet airplane was this big metal bird pressed into forms. Some kind of fan propels it through the sky.

At dawn, there was an announcement to get ready to board. The pale red and yellow rise of the sun masked my future. I shivered as we got on board.

Getting settled into their seats were row after row of strange people of various shapes and sizes. Their eye colors were strikingly different from my own. The colors of their hair and skin—blond hair and white skin, curly black hair and dark skin—also contrasted with mine. Was America their destination, too? The only thing I carried was a white ICM (International Committee for Migration) bag to identify me. I was a pale little boy, small and weightless. Like a child's schoolbag, the ICM bag contained something to eat, a few clothes, and some important documents. I clutched it as if it were a lifeline.

I felt the cool air of the airplane hit my face. People stowed their belongings in small overhead compartments. A stewardess looked at my ticket and directed me to a seat. The orphans were all in different areas of the plane and suddenly, I was alone again. Everything looked spotless and shiny and I was afraid to touch anything. The seat cushion was so soft. A stewardess gave me a pillow! She smiled with sympathy. I gulped at the oxygenated air and almost fainted. I looked for Kim, but couldn't see him. Then I sank into my seat, between two big white men, one of whom smiled and then turned to read his newspaper. The other was preparing to go to sleep.

At that moment, I was overcome with relief at having been rescued from hell as well as anticipation for an entirely new life, one in which I would become the son in my mother's dream.

As we took off, the wings of the plane spread out like the model airplanes of my childhood. I remembered running as I held them high overhead, their propellers twirling. I could almost feel the wind touch my face.

The earth and sky below were vast. Cambodia was covered in fog. I could no longer see it. Beyond the distant sun America was waiting. My eyes filled with tears of joy the more distance there was between my country and myself. I wanted to run and scream and tell everyone on the plane that I had survived. I searched the empty blue sky for my mother's spirit.

I heard a voice calling me. But it was just the stewardess with a tray of food—salad, sandwich, brownie, plastic glass of orange juice. It was heaven. The only problem was that I came from a rice-eating country and I missed the smell of rice. I hoped I wouldn't always have to eat like that in America. I observed how the man next to me was eating the sandwich. I knew few words in English other than "yes" and "no," but the stewardess seemed to understand my nods. I felt like a king. A king who couldn't order rice and was going to a foreign land without a translator.

The salad with French dressing mixed with the brownie and the orange juice and suddenly I had to run to the toilet. I didn't know what to do or where the toilet was. I tried asking the stewardess, but she didn't understand. I gestured to the man next to me but he couldn't understand either. Then I remembered my English lessons. I touched my stomach and said, "Bat-rum." Finally he understood and was kind enough to take me to the lavatory. I thought I was going to mess my pants. Not only was I having an attack of diarrhea, but I needed to pee and felt nauseated. I was about to die. I didn't know food could be so upsetting.

In the bathroom, the light switched on and I was on my own, but I'd never used a toilet in Cambodia. Was I supposed to sit on it with my butt touching the seat, or squat? I decided to do what I used to do back home. I squatted and looked down to make sure I shot straight into the hole. When I finished, I didn't know how to flush. Oh, no! I thought. What do I do? People were waiting to use the bathroom. But I couldn't leave without flushing down my diarrhea. Why wasn't it sinking? Then I remembered the story Thul had told us. If I fell out of the plane, nobody would know. I decided to hold the doorknob with one hand while trying to flush the toilet with the other—if something happened, I could hold on to the door. As my hand was pushing different buttons and signs, the toilet made a loud noise and sucked everything down. Then blue water twirled around the bowl. Oh, no. I pushed the wrong button, I thought. Thul said that if I fell, I would go down into the Atlantic Ocean and be choked by blue saltwater and die. I shut my eyes and held on tightly to the door. Then the toilet silenced and the hole closed up. My forehead was wet with perspiration and my hands and legs were shaky. The next step was to try to get out of the bathroom. I flipped the knob back and forth between "Vacancy" and "Occupied" but the door didn't open. I was in there for almost thirty frightening minutes. Finally, a woman helped me open the door. I decided I would never eat or drink on a plane again.

I thought we were in America when the plane landed. I was so excited that I grabbed my ICM bag and ran through the aisle the moment the plane opened its door to the terminal. When I got out, a security guard said something in English. I pointed forward and said, "America." He asked if he could look into the ICM bag. The bag was how I communicated my needs to people. It was my profile, my personal history, my life, and my interpreter. I felt as if I were deaf and mute. I could not speak, nor could I convey to people what my needs were. People simply looked at the ICM bag and knew exactly what to do. He found that I was an orphaned refugee to be resettled in the United States. He took me back to the plane. We were only in Manila, the Philippines, and the plane was only dropping some passengers off and refueling.

From the Philippines, we flew to San Francisco, a city of lights. My friends had been right. America was heavenly. It was so beautiful that I felt frightened. High-rise buildings, paved roads, and cars were everywhere. I could have never imagined such grandeur. America's vastness spread far and wide below. Cambodia could not compare to it. San Francisco's Bay Bridge stretched out miles away. Houses were made of bricks, stone, and marble. There were no houses on stilts. I would be in a very big city with nothing but buildings and some trees. There were no rice fields anywhere. Where do people farm? I wondered. I felt as if I was in another world, perhaps another planet, inside a star. A powerful deity must have made it all happen and created this beautiful place just for me! It was still a dream. Cambodia came screaming into my head, her pain and anguish a permanent imprint.

This time when the flight attendant made a landing announcement, I wasn't sure whether I should get off. I decided to stay. I wondered where all those Cambodians who were with me in Thailand had gone. Why was I by myself? Where were all the other orphans?

One of the flight attendants came and checked my ICM bag to see where I was supposed to go. The woman had me follow her off the plane and reunited me with the other refugees to be taken to our transfer bus. They were my people, my orphan friends. We spoke the same language. We laughed and felt as if we were real blood brothers. Soon we were being herded onto a bus through a crowd of travelers being welcomed back home from Thailand or the Philippines. Tourists could visit almost everywhere else in Southeast Asia except Cambodia because of the war, land mines, and the Khmer Rouge; Laos and Vietnam didn't allow many tourists either.

We were quarantined for several days in San Francisco before being sent to our assigned destinations. Thick jackets were distributed to us, and we rested and waited for our connecting flights. Most of us had myriad diseases due to many years of nutritional deprivation. We came as a group, but they sent us to various states, to whomever had adopted us. We were bussed back to the airport and taken away to start our new lives.

Kim, one of the orphans from Chunburi camp, was on the plane with me. We were the last to leave San Francisco. Both of us were on our way to New England. I recorded my departure day, June 18, 1982. Our trip took more than six hours, with several connections. The ICM bag was my tongue.

Finally, I arrived at Bradley International Airport near Hartford, Connecticut, my final stop. Again, I sat still and waited until everyone deplaned and the stewardess showed me the way out. She nodded and pointed the way down the aisle, through the jet way, toward the gate where people were waiting to welcome me to their country. I walked slowly and nervously down the square-shaped tube and out into a bright room of smiling faces. I could not speak to my new family. All I did was smile. My new mother was holding up a *Time* magazine with my picture on it. The article had provoked a lot of compassion for the Cambodian orphans. I'd soon learn that my adoptive mother was one of the organizers who brought people's attention to Cambodian children. I was lucky to be in her household, to finally be admitted into her paradise.

My new mother introduced herself and then my new father, brothers, and sisters. They spoke slowly, pointing to themselves as they told me their names. They knew my name but couldn't pronounce it. All I really knew in English was "yes" and "no." But I was their little child. My new mother understood from the article that I had witnessed a lot in my short life. As we drove home, she attempted to tell me different things about their house and the town where we were going to be and pointed to things I should take notice of.

Leaving the airport in the car, I had feelings of joy and horror. I was traveling at the speed of dreams. The highway was smooth asphalt and hundreds of cars seemed to have lives of their own. I had always heard people say that America was a big country where everybody wanted to go. It's big, fun, and has everything you need. I thought all of America would be like San Francisco—a city so vast you can't walk through it in a day. But the town we were going to was so small. It was called Amherst, Massachusetts. At first, I was really disappointed. I had never thought of America as rural. Past the big University of Massachusetts lay a house in the middle of nowhere. We were going into the woods, where it was so quiet. I was nervous as they took me down a dark street.

I had escaped the jungles and now I'm back, lost in the depths of a foreign country. Where are they taking me? I thought to myself.

When we arrived home, my American mother had everything clean and ready for me. She showed me where the bathroom was, how to take a shower, the hot, cold, and warm water, how to wipe myself with the toilet paper, and how to flush the toilet. The moment I saw the toilet bowl, I became frightened. It made a loud, frightening, scary noise every time I flushed it. I was always afraid I would wake people up when I got up in the middle of the night to use the bathroom. I jumped nervously whenever I flushed the toilet.

Everything was so spotless that I felt safe, yet I still felt afraid. I wasn't able to talk to my new brother. We shared a room, but I did not speak his language nor he mine. We just looked at each other. He was day and I was night. Our smiles were awkward and filled with uncomfortable shyness and self-conscious distortions. It was just the beginning.

I hardly slept that first night because I kept waking up to my inner horror. At one point, I woke up and saw my new brother sleeping peacefully. He was snoring, dreaming with assurance of beautiful things. I had to adjust to both the darkness of my fears and the blaze of my hopes and dreams. I wanted to be like him, but it was still too early. I had to get used to this new home and the environment.

Though I was no longer a captive of the Khmer Rouge, I still thought of them often and saw those times in my memory. My dead mother's tears overflowed her eyes. I told her spirit to rest now because I had reached a safe place. I felt that she was happy and that she was free. I had let her go.

My American mother did not look like my own, but I felt that she cared, and that I could depend on her to build my future free of hate and senseless killing. Later, she later told me that the positive kind of revenge I had talked about in Mr. Rosenblatt's *Time* article had been what inspired her to adopt me. All I wanted was to have a good education so that I could honor my mother's wishes. She had wanted me to have a life that inspired others to love peace over war.

TWENTY SIX

A Strange New World

Amherst was smaller than the big city I'd imagined. It didn't have glittering lights and shining skyscrapers or bridges that bent over a vast sea—just a spot of green, with peaches and apples on rolling hills. The forest kept my blond family safe from the world. The smiles and love of my new family slowly lifted my dark cloud. I was scared, but I knew I was safe with them. Like a boat rocked by a soft current, I seemed to float from eye to eye in search of other people's hearts to assure me that I was actually on shore with thousands of miles between me and Cambodia. But it was still incomprehensible as I touched people with large ocean eyes, their lives full of contentment, their abodes filled with unimaginable wealth.

Going to America had not been my original dream. I had thought of France first because of Yean, and because of the familiar French presence in Cambodia. Before I was first interviewed by few months later with the INS man with tattoos. Americans did not come to Cambodia during the dark years of the Khmer Rouge. Only the Chinese were allowed to enter. The Khmer Rouge leader

Pol Pot always had Mao on the tip of his tongue. He wanted his people colored in their own blood through the agrarian revolution he modeled after that of the Chinese. But he had a more blood-thirsty approach than Mao. In the end, the Khmer Rouge could not tell who was who, so they decided to kill whoever was in their way. Sometimes, in my American refuge, I would sit and think of them with hatred. I wanted real revenge, and all my rage came bursting and screaming out. But I remembered my mother's words, to put hate aside and renew my life with the hope that I could one day learn to comprehend everything without hostility.

My American mother spoke to me with her eyes, hands, and smile. She understood that I came from a totally different culture. She was very patient. I was grateful to her for being so kind as to raise someone not of her own flesh. I was a strange little boy, aching with deprivation. My heart resisted her love as I slept each night thinking of my own frail mother being dragged to work by a Khmer Rouge boy. His words echoed in my mind; *You're faking your sickness. Go to work!* At night, I would reach for her to let her know I was OK. "I survived, Mother. Can't you see?" I would whisper, wanting her to touch and feel my flesh and bones. I was the last link to bear her name and her dignity. "I have reached America, Mother. Now it's time for me to heal and express the emotions that I had kept inside of me for such a long time."

Under the Khmer Rouge, no matter how hard life had been, I had always walled up my emotions to keep from falling apart. I had grown numb to everything, even love. Now I had entered a household that offered love on clean plates and clean silver spoons. I did not have to be afraid of being smacked on the head with a ladle when I got my food. In my mind's eye I could see Da as he walked slowly to the communal kitchen to beg for a cup of rice porridge, only to return empty-handed. I could now splash clean faucet water into the Khmer Rouge's hateful, dirty eyes. I had an indoor bathroom and an accessible kitchen where I could have fed Da whatever he desired. I would have loved to see the Khmer Rouge watch him devour good food.

I had a lot of eating to do if I was to grow into a normal-sized body. I was fourteen but still very small, like a little boy. I was prepared to eat just about anything my new mother put on the table. Mashed potatoes with gravy thickened my throat. I swallowed it with a big gulp of water. Salad and bread! I couldn't figure out how to eat raw vegetables with dressing. I had my pick between Ranch and Italian, but I was used to eating boiled vegetables. With my mother's teapot, I had boiled things and it had killed the parasites. Everything in my new home was clean and neatly stacked. Dinner plates were neatly arranged. My American mother and father patiently waited for us to serve ourselves. It was like a family again.

But the food was strange. I had no concept of lasagna, let alone spaghetti, cheese, and crackers. I could not refuse it, though the smell of tomato sauce and cheese was frankly revolting. I yearned for rice. I thought of starvation all over again because I thought it was a kind of starvation to have to eat this kind of food for the rest of my life. It would go into my stomach and stay undigested for days. My new mother had never cooked rice until I came into her life. I began to adjust, to become an American who lives on bread, salad and potatoes, with no rice on his plate. However, the thought of a world without rice filled me with distress. But she eventually figured out that I missed rice, just as I missed my real mother and my pampered childhood and our cuisine. She understood that I was little strange to the food she prepared. After a few weeks, she went to an Asian store and bought a bag of rice, and noodles and soy sauce that I hadn't had for a while, for me to cook myself if I wanted to, since she didn't know how I liked it. Every morning, I woke up early to cook noodles for breakfast. I brought new odors to the house with my Cambodian foods. The aromas of garlic and fish sauce would slip into my parents' room. At times, I didn't want them to know what I was eating. When I ate with them, I would eat very little, but at night, I took Cambodian food into my room and ate it by myself.

I had not put a face to the words "mother" or "father." Since my mother had died, no one had come close to matching the parents who had given birth to me, but I accepted my new American mother. I felt so connected and close to her. I believe that Mother's spirit had guarded me until I found new loving and caring parents who I finally could call Mom and Dad. I did not know what to do or say. They tried by their questions, smiles, and patient formality to make me feel at home.

I was suddenly living at a different level of comfort, surrounded by unfamiliar things. My clothes were washed and dried by machines. My mother folded them neatly and stacked them in a drawer so I could wear them to school the next morning. Dishes, too, were washed by a machine. My real sisters would have been in awe because they would not have had to work so hard around the house if they had such a thing. I couldn't imagine my Cambodian family living like this, in this very comfortable environment, inside a very big house with all these modern things to make life easier and less time consuming. Whenever I needed a bath, I turned on the faucet and water came out like raindrops falling from one spot in a cloud. Toilets, fresh towels, tables, chairs, and elaborate décor surrounded me. Lights and furnace heat, things I could not describe in my own language, had appeared and I didn't know what to do with them.

Everywhere I turned revealed my new family's fortunate position in the world. They had wealth and a life that people everywhere would envy. Yet I could not understand why they had chosen to live so far away from civilization, in the forest where no one could come to visit. In Cambodia, the poor lived in the countryside while the rich lived in cities so they could easily make money and buy things the peasants could never afford. The more wealth a person accumulated the better his position was in society. Whoever lived in the cities had the money and power.

The opposite was true in America, where the rich mostly live in the comfort of peace and isolation far from the city traffic and fumes. I only discovered later that my family had wealth beyond those who dwelled in the urban slums of my new country. Television news showed American city dwellers begging passersby for spare change.

I was taken out of my violent world into a family of smiles. Like a mute, I took in their kindness through my eyes. My sisters and brothers were well prepared to think of me as if I belonged there. I fought with my sister over the television just as if she had been one of my regular siblings. I wanted to watch my kung fu movies and she wanted to watch *Little House on the Prairie*. We struggled over the remote control, but I usually got my way. It was my home now, too, and I had the right to watch whatever shows I wished. There was only one television, though, and my sister probably resented my presence, as I had invaded her home and could be stubborn.

One thing that was very difficult getting used to was the toilet. Sometimes, I sneaked out in the middle of the night to piss or shit outside. In the dark, I sat between bushes in the backyard. It was more comfortable than sitting on the toilet inside the house. I also felt embarrassed because my sisters were sleeping in a room right next to the bathroom. I didn't want them to hear me whenever I had to go, so I went outside, sometimes even when I was afraid of the dark. In the morning, I would get up very early to go to the bathroom outside. The natural environment suited my habits and, just like when I was in Cambodia, I used leaves for toilet paper. Mother started to get curious about why I woke up so early every morning. Then one morning, she followed me to see what I was doing. Was I practicing a praying ritual? she wondered. Then she found out that I was using the outdoors as my pissing ground. Mother must have told Father to give me indoor bathroom lessons. "Toilet," he said, pointing to it. "Sit like this. Outside, no pee. Inside toilet." My twin sisters giggled. Father demonstrated all over again the use of the bathtub, the shower, obtaining hot and cold water, the twist of the faucet, the shiny sink in which to wash my face. When it seemed I still wasn't understanding it, he called on a Cambodian social worker.

I had not seen another Cambodian since I'd arrived at my new home. A sense of excitement rippled through me in anticipation of meeting the social worker who was coming to explain what I needed to do in my own language.

"My name is Sovann Doung," he said in Khmer on the day we met. He was about twenty-one years old, tall, and dark-skinned. He spoke English fluently. I wished I could speak and understand it as well as he did. I was very excited speaking Khmer to him.

"Call me Sovann or older brother (Bong), either one is OK," he said.

Day after day, I had been in my room, trapped in my silent world. I *wanted* to hear Khmer spoken again. I hadn't truly communicated with anyone in the house. I missed the rice fields and the people who looked like me. Sovann spoke in his soft voice, smiling at the thought of what he had been told by my new mother and father. Sovann took me to the kitchen, along with my mother and father, and asked what I was doing outside the house every morning, as if I had committed a great sin.

"I went to take a shit," I told him. Although we had never met before, Sovann laughed as if it was our shared secret. It was like some ritual we all did together out in the bushes of Cambodia. Only Cambodians would understand.

"What did he say?" Mom asked Sovann, her anxious eyes all lit up for the translation. Once she understood, she was the next to laugh.

"No, no," she said, shaking her head, still laughing. "In this country, people don't go to the bathroom outside." She tried to tell me that I was civilized now, with modern conveniences for my use, and didn't have to go outside anymore. What a great thing that was. I could just sit on the toilet and let all my poop drop into the water and, like magic, flush it down, and I wouldn't have to worry about where it all ended up.

"Oh," I resisted. "But the bathroom is so clean. I don't want to dirty it. I don't feel comfortable sitting on that shiny thing. I never used one before." Sovann translated. "Except in the airplane."

In addition to helping me acclimate to "modern conveniences," Sovann opened the doors to other possibilities, new kinds of camaraderie. He offered me shared experiences, laughter, and reminiscences of Cambodia. Sovann understood what it meant to be a displaced orphan from the land where Cambodians killed Cambodians. He took me out of my comfortable American home into the less formal place of a Cambodian home with walls dirtied by children's fingers smearing mud. The smell of Khmer cooking, barbecued ribs, and curry brought all my Khmer senses back after the months of Italian and American food I had consumed with great resistance.

A few months after I settled in with my new family, more Cambodian orphans arrived to live with American families in Amherst. We exchanged telephone numbers so that we could talk through the wires about our lives and needs. We wanted to ease our loneliness and loosen our American tongues. I had been wondering where all the orphans I had lived with in Khao-I-Dang had gone. I found some of them in Amherst. Every week, the friends I made would rendezvous for movies and chitchat.

I was having trouble adjusting, though. At times, I resented my new parents for expecting me to ask for everything, even for permission to go out and have fun. In Cambodia I'd had to grow into adulthood early and become independent to survive. I had been accountable only to myself for everything I did. But my American parents made rules they expected me to follow, which I resisted. It was so hard to adapt to their structures and rules, but no matter what, I felt I had to respect my new parents because they were the ones giving me a new life of hope. They wanted to know where I was going and when I would be back home. At dinner time; I was expected to be on time and silently pray for a few seconds with the family. Asking permission was not in my vocabulary, so it was hard, when I made friends and wanted to hang out with them, to have to tell my parents about it. I felt it wasn't their business. I was my own man in an orphan boy's skin, and I felt I could do whatever I wanted, the way I always had, alone on the streets of Phnom Penh and surviving the wreckage of war.

I was sick of rules, and anyone who seemed to encroach on my freedom enraged me. In response, I would see a Khmer Rouge face in a flashback and that summoned all my anger, ready for a kill. To get calm again, I had to concentrate and find the child in me that my mother had loved. With my American family, I never really knew what to expect or how to behave. Everything was proper, ordered, formal, and different from what I was used to. Even the way people sat, ate, talked, and dressed made me feel awkward, as if I was being "civilized" out of backwardness.

I was surprised by something else, too. For the first time, I witnessed people expressing affection toward each other. My new parents kissed each other on the lips and my sisters on the forehead to say good night. I had never seen my biological parents kiss each other. My real father had always been distant. It was his man's role. My mother had always been intimate with us, but by means of her smiles, her angelic delicacy, and the way she watched over us to make sure that we were well fed. My father had always been able to count on her to be a traditional woman. Suddenly, people were hugging and kissing. I felt odd seeing it.

I was embarrassed for my sisters when they wore swimsuits. I felt they should wear long sarongs to cover their legs and conceal every part of their bodies underneath the dark fabric. When we went swimming, I didn't want other people to know they were my sisters. I stayed away from them and when we were waiting for our parents to pick us up, they weren't sure what was the matter with me. I acted strange toward them, quiet and distant.

I was unable to express my feelings. I had learned to keep my anger, my sadness, and my depression to myself. My new parents would ask, "How are you this morning?" and I would reply, "Fine," and smile outwardly, but I was not fine on the inside. I didn't want my American parents to worry. I was still in the mind-set of staying alive. I didn't want sorrow to get in the way of finding food.

I didn't want to feel sorry for myself. If I told others what I was feeling, I might be exposed the way my twin sisters were exposed in their swimsuits.

I had always believed that you have to solve your own problems. Therefore, it was useless to confide in anyone what I was thinking or feeling. I worried that if I told people about my problems, I would cause *them* troubles, and if my new parents became upset or annoyed with me, they might send me back to the refugee camp. My real mother had always said, "Respect the people who are caring for you. Be grateful to them and don't cause them problems or grief." I was always the good boy my mother wanted me to be. When I felt sad or angry, I went to my room and shut the door. I could not open up to my new parents and my new family.

However, it got easier as time went on. My parents allowed me the time and space to make adjustments. They understood why I was behaving in certain ways. They had read about it in magazines and books, and Sovann had probably provided them with an understanding of our culture. For a wounded child, doctors prescribed patience and compassion. In time, as I learned and became more fluent in the culture of my new parents, I began to feel more at ease sharing things with them. Little by little, I learned to express my feelings.

One day I couldn't figure out why my dad was so upset when he was talking to me. I though I was showing him respect by looking down, without making eye contact. He took that as an insult because he didn't understand my culture. He was getting angrier because I refused to look at him in the American way when he was disciplining me. He wanted me to look him straight in the eyes while he was talking to me. I kept looking away and down. He thought I was being disrespectful, but I had meant well and was fearful of being spanked. My real father would have whipped me if had I been a bad boy. It took me a while to understand the new rules and traditions. My American father meant well. He was a very strong, handsome man, and a gentle soul. He wasn't aware of

Cambodian culture, so we both made mistakes that upset both of us. I felt ashamed because I had made my father angry. He yelled, but I kept my distance and inwardly I was praying for his compassion. He later apologized, which my real father would never have done, and hugged me to show his love, another thing my father would never have done. My father would have spanked me and that would be the end of the matter, with no discussion or emotion.

Once I got used to the ways of my American parents, I took their love with ease and gratitude. They had kept physical violence out of the family and raised their children to become good people without inflicting additional wounds. In some ways, they understood where I was coming from. They took the time to learn about my experiences.

I eventually learned to thrive in this new environment. With the teachings of my birth parents to guide me, I learned how to survive, endure, and respect the life I have.

In his article in *Time* on January 11, 1982, Roger Rosenblatt had talked about my survival story during the Khmer Rouge regime and my mother's last request to avenge her when the country was back to normal. My American mother had been influenced by this story and went from church to church to encourage people in the Connecticut River Valley to adopt Cambodian orphans. Many of them became my friends. As more orphans resettled with American families, I had more friends who spoke the same language. Most of them were homesick and suffering from culture shock like me. Every time we gathered, we talked about how we missed our food, homeland, family, and experiences. We talked about our problems living with American families and about our schoolwork. Most of us were later diagnosed with post-traumatic stress disorder (PTSD). We had to learn to cope by talking to our American parents, who knew very little about our experiences. We tried to keep ourselves busy by joining sports in school and other activities outside of school. We became attached to each other like brothers and sisters. Since then we have gone on to succeed as engineers, educators, and computer scientists. I am very proud of my orphan friends. We struggled together and finally succeeded in our goals. Now we have a chance to help our native country in its ongoing struggles. We were born together and we still share a painful past that we will never forget.

TWENTY SEVEN

My American Dream

My first summer in America, 1982, I was happy and safe under that crisp, blond-haired and blue-eyed sky of my American home. It was hot outside, but never as hot was it can be in Cambodia. The heat of my old country stayed in my memory as I experienced this changing weather. How strange it was to see people lying outdoors in the sun, baking themselves brown! In Cambodia, people wanted to be white, but these Americans wanted dark, peasant skin. My light Chinese skin had been cause for suspicion among the Khmer Rouge. They had tried to make me a peasant and had tested my endurance to see how much I could take, living without food and working for them nonstop, day and night, sweating in the hot weather. Amherst was a world of sun away from all the dark hatred of my past. I wanted to lie with these sunbathers to darken myself, perhaps to secure my own sense of place in the warmth of a relaxing afternoon. It was my first time seeing people stretched out leisurely in the sun, in their bareness, in shorts and bikinis, while the flying wind sent chills over my conservatively covered body. How lonely I felt not to be able to talk about these surprises.

One morning after breakfast, my father filled his trailer with camping supplies. I was not sure what camping was. I looked it up in a Khmer-English dictionary but still couldn't understand it. It seemed that we were going to a jungle, far away from human civilization. Father was gentle and kind, but clueless about the world in which I had lived. The memory of the evacuation suddenly came to me and I thought I was leaving for good for another unfamiliar place. My twin sisters, meanwhile, were gleeful at the thought of leaving to explore the forest far away. I was not pleased when Mother motioned them to gather their things. That much I understood. Her expression called for obedience. While all the commotion was happening, I sat at the kitchen table waiting to see what would happen next. My mother beckoned me with her hand, gesturing for me to pack my own clothes. She held up one of my sisters' suitcases as a way of communicating that I, too, needed to go upstairs and pack my things. I did not understand, but I ran upstairs. In my room, I sat politely waiting for further instructions, with music playing on my headphones. I heard a knock on my door. I opened it and Father stood there smiling. He motioned with his hand: "Let's go." I was not ready. My clothes were not packed. Father reached for a suitcase and started to pack for me. I thought that I must have done something wrong.

Where was he taking me? I wondered. Nevertheless, I knew that he was a nice man and a father I could count on to keep me from danger. I went along and trusted in the journey for as long as the ride took, watching every passing scene and picturesque landscape. Trees and mountains were a vast dreamland. I never imagined it would happen this way, but there I was, with happy little sisters in the backseat of the station wagon singing childhood songs they'd learned from books and television. We traveled on a highway surrounded by trees and gorges, mountains, crevices, and rocks all colored with earth and so beautiful and natural they stirred in me a sense of fear. In my memory, the jungle was somewhere dark and wild and dangerous, with flesh-eating animals lying in wait. The idea of camping in the middle of nowhere was very strange. Yet I felt protected in the company of strangers whom I was learning to know and love. Father found a very beautiful spot on which to set up our tents before dark. Mother prepared food while my sisters played in their tent.

Why here? I kept thinking. Are they all crazy? They have a house, with beds to sleep in, electricity, tables and chairs, a nice kitchen to cook in, and a lot of food in the fridge. Why in the world are they here in this forest, sleeping in tents and cooking with small utensils? If I had spoken English, I would have asked them to turn the trailer around and go back home. Camping was too much like the Cambodia I left. To my family, though, it was a paradise, an escape from the chaos of civilization and the routine work of their lives. I thought they were out of their mind crazy and I couldn't believe that they enjoyed a vacation in the jungle instead of going to the city.

I camped with them for a whole week, imagining certain kinds of life-threatening danger. My parents did not know that I took a knife into my tent as a form of protection. I was still afraid of wild animals—boars, tigers, and snakes—the sound of critters in the dark. I laid low to hide myself from imaginary thieves and soldiers. A week of camping seemed like a year. When it was camping time again the following year, I refused to go. I preferred to stay home in my comfortable bed, or lounging on the couch with my music and TV. The luxuries of life had made me like the son of a king and a queen. Only later would I understand that camping is a peaceful break, a vacation, a time to think, a time to decide one's purpose in this world.

When I first arrived in Amherst, the school year was coming to an end for summer vacation. I was disappointed not to be able to start school right away, and my parents had to persuade me that "learning" is not something one does only in school. They said they would help me learn many things of value during the summer.

But as September finally approached, the thought of school both excited and frightened me. Mother had told me that education was the best revenge I could take against the world of evil. But it had been a long time since I had gone to school, and I had forgotten so much. During the time of the Khmer Rouge, I had to hide what I knew, especially the fact that I could read and write. The Khmer Rouge silenced our minds, our hearts, and our curiosity. They extinguished our questions and the need to explore and understand who we were and where we lived. How could I go back to school? I would have to learn everything afresh.

"You're going to school with me tomorrow," my new mother said. "Don't worry, you'll make friends." Still, I was worried; how would the other children perceive me? Would they like me? I was told that there would be other Cambodian orphans at school. I could not wait to be reunited with them again.

Mom and Dad accompanied me to the main office to register. They filled out papers and forms. Then they left me in the guidance office. I sat gazing at people rushing in and out of the hallway and going from one classroom to the next. The first ring of a bell called them out of one classroom. By the second ring they were in another. The sounds of walking and talking put me in a dismal state. I searched for each classroom on my own, guided only by a schedule I could not read. I remembered being back in Cambodia, hearing the crickets in the night and feeling the sadness of being alone. Now I was in a different kind of jungle with gibbons screaming in my ears, haunting me. I couldn't hear my mother's voice because I was too busy trying to listen to the students passing me by as if I were invisible. The large hallway opened wide and students disappeared into their classrooms. I stared at my class schedule, wondering where I was supposed to be, trying to decipher the number on each door I passed and looking to see if I would be welcomed inside. Someone found my homeroom for me, and I was shoved in among white students who acted indifferently to my presence. When the bell rang, everyone left for their other classes.

I didn't understand why. In Cambodia we would stay in the same classroom all day. I sat there until my teacher had someone show me to another class.

I felt so alone among people who looked nothing like me. There were a few students with eyes like mine, but they didn't understand what I had been through. They, too, passed me by, without any "Hi" or "What's up?" These slanted-eyed Asians were born American, with the English language in their blood. They did not want to speak to me because I was new and could not understand their language. They left me to my fear and confusion, wanting so desperately to fit into their sheltered world. This school had a roof, tiled floor, and bricks, all designed and constructed so that the students could learn in comfort. It had a library full of books and learning materials, classrooms full of desks and tables that filled me with awe. It was so different from school in Cambodia, where we wrote each letter with chalk on our little blackboards as the teacher called out the alphabet, and raised the blackboards up high so she could see how we had written it. Knowledge was memorized by heart. The same memorization, if it could be retained, was to be passed down from one generation to the next.

Everyone became silent when I walked into my earth science class late because I couldn't find the room. My face was blank and my heart racing as I met their stares. "What is your name?" my teacher asked. I could feel everyone looking at me with their beautiful eyes, long noses, and brown-colored hair, their fair skin so different from my own. They assumed I was Chinese unless I was introduced as a Cambodian. My teacher did just that, apologizing for mispronouncing my name, asking other students to welcome me since I would be spending the school year with them. I didn't understand what she was saying, but I gave her a smile, acknowledging her supreme status. I felt as though I was on display. My only means of communication was my smile and a nod. I hoped that my smile showed that I respected them. I always kept in mind that I should never cause them any trouble or worry. I felt like I was a jungle boy coming to live in the modern world. Most of the time, I withdrew into silence, learning through observation how to make my way in the American world.

I didn't have to make a lot of effort to understand math. I was good at it. It was visual and either right or wrong. In the refugee camp, I had learned fractions already and whizzed through the pre-test while other students struggled with it. In my new math class, I was the only Asian person among white students, who now thought of me as the great mathematician of the East. Nevertheless, I went from one class to the next with such discomfort and nervousness that I wanted to give it all up. I had no friends, so I drew a curtain around myself and shut everybody out. I thought American children were crazy, like wild reeds swayed by the wind. They were very aggressive, the way they talked and the way they walked, compared to Cambodians. Cambodian children are not supposed to talk back to older people, for example, and boys and girls do not openly hug or kiss their friends. Americans were free. They danced with one another at school. It was a great shock to me, but no teachers punished them. They didn't seem embarrassed. I envied them for their free spirit, their fearless assertiveness, and their sense of being carefree. They had everything: parents, a nice house, a car, and people all around them telling them, "I love you." They thrived in an environment of peace and prosperity, but they didn't seem to notice—what they had was like second nature to them. Their freedom was expected. It was something they were born to have and felt entitled to.

I wished I had a voice to speak. I wanted to tell them where I had been and what I had seen. That was the wall between them and me, although we were the same age. My tongue was tied out of fear of not speaking English properly. English was gibberish, mumbo-jumbo. I wanted so badly to succeed, but I couldn't understand what my teachers were communicating, especially when they gave homework assignments.

What they taught at school went in one ear and out the other. Their lips moved, but I was a deaf-mute. I couldn't understand anything they said. I was very impatient, because I wanted so eagerly to become an American. When I couldn't learn fast enough, I began to doubt my ability to make it through school at all. I had missed so many years of education and now had so many to go. It was very frustrating, and I expressed a lot of anger towards myself and, occasionally, towards my teachers and parents as well.

Although I made A's and B's, I was never good at taking exams. I was always the last one to finish. Sometimes I gave up and left a test unfinished. But the strange sounds of English were slowly starting to sink in. I stayed after school every day to get special tutoring, and at home Mom and Dad explained my homework by pointing things out with gestures. Their patience and perseverance made the difference between learning English and not learning it.

Once I learned the language, I excelled. In high school I was on top of the world. And my American parents deserve a lot of credit for that feeling. I had become toughened by the demands of going to school when I felt completely different from the other students. I learned to walk with confidence against the ridicule of other kids, who called me the Chinese or Jap who knew karate. At a basketball game, I was ready to take on boys twice my size for unnecessarily fouling me. I learned to be aggressive, like the others. I was no longer shy and passive. With my new linguistic skills, I cursed in English and returned taunts whenever I could. I was ready to hurt anyone who got in my way, no matter how big and tough they were. I didn't care if a guy was six feet tall or twice my size. Unfortunately, I had the teachings of the Khmer Rouge in my blood. The guys who tried to pick on me didn't know that.

One day I couldn't take being a nice person anymore. In the hallway of my high school, I came upon a football player who owed me money for a drum set I had sold him, and I jumped up to punch him in the face. He turned and tried to defend himself. His face turned red and he swore at me. He was about to pounce on me, but I guess he saw the anger in my face and stopped. I moved a couple of steps away from him and yelled in broken English. Then I leapt up very high like a kick boxer and hit him right in the face. The crowd surrounded me, cheering in the hallway. I got my moment of fame for being a fearless little creature. In my mind, I'd inherited my strength from Bruce Lee, descendent of Asiatic invaders, and I was going to out box the white Chuck Norris. The principal called my foster parents so I could explain the problem to them. Afterward, no one dared come close to me and no one called me names. "He knows martial arts," they would whisper, and they resolved never to mess around with the serious little guy.

In 1987, I entered the University of Massachusetts at Amherst. I had worked hard to get there. There were times when I had doubts. But then I remembered my mother's words that I had to take advantage of the opportunity, and to respect and honor those who cared for me. No matter how hard life seemed, I knew it was better than what I'd had before. Despite my times of doubt, America provided a safe refuge, an opportunity to shape my own life, to fight for what I believe is important, and to find ways to channel grief into fruitful action. I was free now to soar, and nothing was going to stop me from taking my rightful flight in the world of my American dream.

Epilogue

I now live the dream that occupied my thoughts as a young refugee boy. There are many reasons why I love the United States of America. To begin with, it is a place of choice, where I have had the opportunity to make myself the person that I want to be. I have an education, a home, a job that I love, a family of my own, a car to drive, and physical and mental security that allow me to go wherever I wish. Freedom is priceless and I would not trade it for anything in the world. Four of us survived. My sister Theary escaped in the early 1980's to a refugee camp in Thailand and several years later she got sponsored to Sweden. My two other siblings San and Chan are living in Cambodia. We have between us given my parents eleven grandchildren.

When I was a young child, before the Khmer Rouge, my parents brought me to the Pagoda for special Buddhist holidays. I observed (and learned) from the monks while they gave spiritual blessings, chanted, and guided us with their gentleness and kindness. I helped my mother bring fruit, flowers, and basic supplies to the monks. I brought incense, candles, and lotus flowers, and I placed them in front of the Buddha statues. I folded my hands in front of my face, praying that I would be a good boy. I sat quietly in the same manner as my parents and I watched the monks as they chanted peacefully. My parents explained to me that the paintings on the walls and ceiling of the temple depicted heaven and hell. My parents taught me the importance of compassion, care, and respect. They raised me to be a good person.

When my mother wrestled with her last breath, she spoke to me of revenge. "Education," she said, "is the best revenge you can have." Then she left me alone in a cold world of hatred and violence that almost completely transgressed the vitality of the human spirit. When I was orphaned, I became a child of the revolution. The Khmer Rouge took ownership of my soul and of my body. I was not allowed to have emotions or to show sadness at the death of others, even my parents or siblings. The Khmer Rouge sought to purify the minds of children so that they could use us to harm others. But as hard as they tried, the Khmer Rouge could not erase the memory and impact of my wonderful parents.

I knew that the Khmer Rouge were wrong and evil, and I was determined never to join them. The totality of my childhood made me a stronger person and even more determined to do good for others. I was —and am still— at peace, knowing that my mother did not leave my side during my childhood in the jungle. She never left me. Her presence, in both life and death, has guided, soothed, and helped me to cope with trauma. My mother and her ghost spirit have been important keys to my survival.

It was my mother's wish for me to make something of my life without causing suffering for others. This is what she meant by "revenge."

I can never forgive the Khmer Rouge for the deaths of my parents, brothers and sisters, and the pain they forced me to endure. And I have no power, right, or desire to take up arms and seek out those who killed my family. The cycle of hatred can only end with what I do to prevent such atrocities in the future. Telling my story is an important part of helping me cope with my experiences and the trauma of witnessing bloody horrors that turned into nightmares, then to memories, but never leave.

"Positive revenge" heals me so that I can positively influence others. I have a moral obligation to live well, as a statement about the human spirit, about what matters and about what we can do in this world of suffering. Suffering has demanded that I be better than myself.

I tell my story with the hope that others can learn from it. For me, revenge means forgiveness, education, and positive actions. It means moral courage, based on wisdom acquired over time. Every part of our life's experience needs to be reflected upon.

It has been over 30 years. I have accomplished my American dream. I have a job, home and my own family. I have been working as an educator in Lowell's public schools for twenty years. I am not only a guidance counselor, but a public speaker, recounting to students every year my story of survival when I was of middle school age.

It is wonderful to read what these children say about how my message affects them. I know that they listen, because when they write to me they tell me what they remember from my talk, particularly that I was their age when these things happened to me, and how I survived the cruelty. They write that my story has an effect on their own lives. This impact makes it worth sharing my story. These are letters from six graders written to me.

"Dear Mr. Ty,

The story that you told us inspired me that I can make it through my life. If I had to pick someone to be my friend, it would be you because I like to hear about your life. You inspired me in all kinds of way. I think you took a piece of my heart in that story. I wish you had your family back, because I know how it feels when you lose a family member. If only I could write the book for you, that would be great, but that is okay. I wouldn't mind hearing your story every day of my life. I bet you inspired everyone, even the teachers. I think you inspired me the most. But one thing I don't understand why they treated you so badly. I wish there were no more war so the world would come to peace. Well, thank you for the inspiring story that you told everyone.

Your friend,

Shane

Dear Mr. Ty,

I am Matthew, a ninth grader from Innovation Academy Charter School in Chelmsford, Massachusetts. My school recently held the Camp Darfur genocide awareness event that you attended. I would like to thank you so much for coming and sharing your incredible story of your life in Cambodia. Under the Khmer Rouge. It was truly a powerful account that I will never forget.

Before my school starting teaching us about genocides. I had little knowledge of what the Cambodian genocide was. That soon changed but there are still many people in the world that are not aware of the terrors that occurred in Cambodia while the Khmer Rouge was in power. I think it great that you go around telling your story to people so that not only will they know about the atrocities that took place , but also they will never forget them either.

Your story touched me deeply. You are an incredible person to have come from living on the streets in Cambodia to teaching at a school all the way across the world. Your determination and resilience is an inspiration to me as it should be to anyone who hears your story.

Thank you so much for coming to our Camp Darfur event and telling your story. It was so powerful I will carry it with me for the rest of my life. I am eternally grateful for everything you have done to spread awareness of the terror of genocide.

Sincerely,

Matthew

And,

Dear Mr. Ty,

First of all, I would like to thank you for taking time and talking to us in the sixth grade about your courageous adventure of escaping from Cambodia. I think that you were a very strong and courageous boy to stand all the pain when you were little. Your story was very touching and even made me cry! I think it was very brave of you to sneak into the rice fields and steal food so that you wouldn't have to starve. I imagine one of the scariest times for you was when your mom, dad, and brother died. But how you got through all of that and decided to come to America on a plane was very brave of you. It was also very funny when you told us about the time when you went to the bathroom on the plane, and were scared of falling into the ocean with no one noticing. I think it is great that you took time to tell children about your courageous adventure. I think your story should be published in the newspapers or maybe you should write a book.

Sincerely,

Jasmine

My older child is now beginning to ask me questions about my childhood. For the sake of my children, and all these other children, I have now written this book.

Dedication

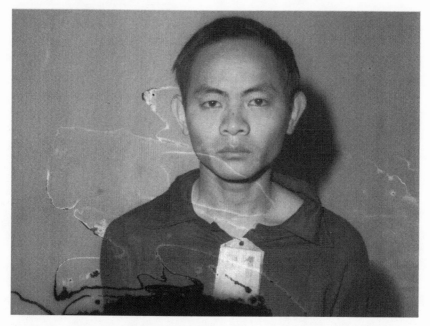

My oldest brother Yean in the Tuol Sleng prison. Thousands of Cambodian intellectuals were killed in Tuol Sleng.

I dedicate this book to the memory of my brother Yean, who was a gentle, kind and hard working person. He was our family role model for us to follow in his footsteps. His life was filled with hope and dreams of success in his higher education in France. He was one of the top ranking students in Cambodia and received a full scholarship to study engineering in France in 1971. Four years later, he had completed his education and returned to visit the family in 1974. It was a big event and our family was filled with joy in celebrating his accomplishments. I will always remember my last glimpse of him as we said goodbye before he walked into the plane taking him back to France.

Three years later, Yean arrived in Cambodia on the dark, dark day of July 5, 1977. He had been tricked by Brother No 3

Ieng Sary who was foreign minister in the Khmer Rouge regime. He publicly urged Yean and other Cambodians living abroad to return home, claiming they were wanted and needed by the revolutionary government to help rebuild their country. Yean was hoping to reunite with family members that he hadn't heard from since he left. In reality, he, like all the others students who returned from abroad, was arrested as soon as he landed at Pochentong International Airport and transported to the secret prison Tuol Sleng. This photograph captures his sadness and hopelessness before they took his life.

Acknowledgements

I wish to thank my mother, father and other family members long dead, whose spirits have always inspired me, strengthened me and kept me going throughout the years. My mother's spirit helped and guided me to find a new home and a new mother in America—a country I had only dreamed about. I'll forever hold in my heart the memories of my mother— never forgetting all our times together. My mother has empowered me to be the strong person I am today, succeeding to fulfill her wishes. I have shed many tears in sorrow and happiness with you, my loved ones. You left me before I was nine years old, and even after all these years, I feel I have not done enough to repay the respect you gave me. You gave me life and you raised me to be a strong person. I dedicate this book to you and our family. I leave this book for your grandchildren, so they will know your pain and suffering through my testimony.

I honor everyone who has lost someone to the brutality of Cambodia's Khmer Rouge regime. I hope they will keep their loved ones' memories alive as I have tried to do in this book. I hope they share their experiences with their children and grandchildren so they will know the atrocities in Cambodia's history.

I am thankful for those of my family who did survive—my sisters Theary and Chan, my brother San and my cousin Thisy Kim. We share a bond which can never be expressed in words. We have been to the dark side and somehow managed to come through to the light.

Words alone will never express the thanks and love I hold for my adopted American family, Marlena and Tracy Tumlin, Richard Brown and Marget Sands, Amy Ferguson, Julie Kenner, Raymond Kenner, Bethany Brown, Joia Brown, Noelle Brown and Andrea Brown, who helped design this beautiful book cover. You all gave me my life back. You gave me a future. You gave me hope. You saved me physically and emotionally.

My heart will always be with my orphan friends who had survived the killing fields: Thy Oeur, Boreth Sun, Chuck Sath, Hong Cheng, Chantha and Reymond Bin, Hai Cheng, Hong Net, Khoun Loeun, Roeun Chea, Arn Chorn-Pond and many other orphans who survived but aren't listed in this book. We thrive.

Many thanks to people who helped and inspired me writing this memoir: Janice Russel, Francis Murphy, Fred and Quesen Brown. And to Chath Piersath, Michael Jan Friedman, Steve Glauber, Christopher Martin, Tooch Van, Professor Lorraine Cordeiro, Susan Pickford, Janice Russell, Jackie Travers, Dennis W. Hallinan, Sue Alexander, Chip Chaunamom, Mary Fitzhugh and the Kirkus Review for editing this book. I want to thank Yourk Chhang, Director of the Documentation Center of Cambodia, for providing a photograph of my brother from Tuol Sleng, and James Higgins for designing this book.

To Roger Rosenblatt, Neil Boothby and Matthew Naythons a very special thanks you. I will be forever grateful that you talked to me in that Thai refugee camp so many years ago and included my story and photographs in your Time magazine article in 1982. Your insightful journalism opened doors for me in America I never would have thought possible. I am honored you included me in your book *Children of War*. Thank you for your compassion and kindness and for taking the time to write the foreword to this book.

And lastly, to my wonderful wife, Sreymom, and my two beautiful children, Ethan and Sofia. You will forever have my heart. Thank you for supporting me in everything I do, for making my life so happy and complete.

For more information or to order additional copies of The Years of Zero for your school or institution, please contact or visit the author's website.

Website: www.sengty.com

Email: yearsofzero@sengty.com

Made in the USA
Charleston, SC
27 March 2014